Adventures in
SNAP!
Programming

Learn to design exciting
and challenging programs

Abhay B. Joshi

Published by:
SPARK Institute and Publications
16668 NE 121st ST
Redmond, WA 98052 USA
1st edition: 5 October 2020

To order your copy:
Go to Amazon.com
Or write to: abjoshi@yahoo.com

Cover design by
Ravindra Pande

Other books in this series:
http://www.abhayjoshi.net/spark/csseries.pdf

Background

"Snap!" is a programming language that is based on MIT's Scratch. You can run it in any web browser by using the link http://snap.berkeley.edu. In the subsequent discussion I am going to call it "Snap" (instead of "Snap!").

The idea of using *computer programming as a medium for learning* is rapidly gaining acceptance. The benefits of learning programming and *computer science* concepts well before college – even in elementary grades – are well-understood.

Here is a list of some of the amazing things that happen when students engage in computer programming:

- Students become *active* and *creative* learners, because they explore ideas through a hands-on activity with an infinitely powerful tool.
- They learn to think about and analyze *their own thinking*, because that is the only way to program computers.
- They learn to solve complex problems by breaking them into smaller sub-problems.
- They learn a new way of thinking (called "computational" thinking).
- In the world of programming, answers are not simply "right" or "wrong"; this prepares a student's mindset for real-life problems.
- Students' learning processes are transformed from *acquiring facts* to *thinking creatively and analytically*

About this book

Snap is a powerful language and offers access to lots of advanced ideas of Computer Science some of which are appropriate for a college-level programming course.

There is a lot of material on Snap Programming on the Internet, including videos, online courses, projects, and so on, but, most of it is introductory. There is very little that can take students to the next level, where they can apply their Snap and CS concepts to exciting and challenging problems. There is also very little material that shows students how to design complex projects, and introduces them to the process of programming.

In short:
- This book is for students who are already familiar with Snap – its various commands, and its user interface – and basic CS concepts such as, variables, conditional statements, looping, and so on.
- The book attempts to teach students how to "design" programs through a series of challenging and interesting projects on science simulation, games, puzzles, and math problems.

Where to learn Snap and CS concepts

The projects covered in this book are all based on a variety of CS and Snap concepts. This book does not attempt to explain these concepts. If you are a newcomer to Snap and/or CS, I recommend to you my other book "**Learn CS Concepts with Snap**".

What is in the book?

I have organized the book as a series of independent Snap projects – each of which describes how to design and build an interesting and challenging Snap program. Each project progresses in stages – from a simple implementation to increasingly complex versions. You can take up these projects in any order you like, although I have tried to arrange them in an increasing order of challenge.

Programming is a powerful tool that can be applied to virtually any field of human endeavor. I have tried to maintain a good diversity of applications in this book. You will find the following types of projects:

- Arcade games
- Puzzle games
- Simulations

- Math games
- Geometric designs
- Optical illusions

Learn the concepts through application

As the experts will tell you, concepts are really understood and internalized when you apply them to solve problems. The purpose of this book is to help you apply Snap and CS concepts to solve interesting and challenging programming problems. Every chapter lists, at the very start, the Snap and CS concepts that you will apply while building that project.

Learn the design process

Besides these technical concepts, you will also learn the "**divide and conquer**" approach of problem-solving. This is a fancy term for the technique of breaking down a bigger problem into many smaller problems and solving them separately one by one.

You will learn a bit about a program design technique called "**object-oriented thinking**". Without going into its gory details such as *classes* and *inheritance*, the book tries to show you how you can view each program as a collection of independent objects that cooperate to deliver a coherent experience.

You will also learn the "**iterative design process**" for designing programs. This is another fancy name that describes the idea that something complex can be designed in a repeated *idea -> implement -> test* cycle, such that in each cycle we add a little more complexity.

Finally, you will learn a bit of "**project management**". Project management helps you undertake a project – such as painting your house, celebrating your sister's birthday, or creating a complex computer program – and complete it in a reasonable time, with reasonable effort, and with reasonable quality. It involves things such as planning tasks, tracking their progress, etc. When you undertake the programming projects in this book, you will learn some of these project management techniques.

Audience for the book

The book is intended for students who are already familiar with Snap. The level of challenge is tuned for high-school students and above, but middle-school students who have picked up all the concepts in an introductory course might also be able to enjoy the projects presented in this book.

The book would be a great resource for teachers who teach Snap programming. They could use the projects to teach advanced tricks of programming and to show how complex programs are designed.

Finally, the book is for anyone who wants to get the wonderful taste of the entertaining and creative aspect of Computer Programming.

Hardware/software and program files

You can do all your Snap programming work online by creating your own account at http://snap.berkeley.edu.

The scripts of every project in this book can be seen in the link given at the end of every chapter. In addition, there are starter files and intermediate program versions, all of which are available free of cost upon request: please write to me at my email address below.

If you purchased a printed copy of this book, all images would be gray. The color images (organized by chapter) are available for free download at: http://abhayjoshi.net/spark/snap/book3/images.zip.

Abhay B. Joshi (abjoshi@yahoo.com)
Seattle, USA
5 October 2020

Acknowledgements

I wish to thank Tanuja Joshi for reviewing the material of this book diligently and tirelessly and for providing me with valuable suggestions. I wish to thank Ravindra Pande for creating a truly beautiful cover for the book.

I wish to thank TEALS (https://www.tealsk12.org) – a nonprofit organization dedicated to the cause of teaching computer science to all high school students – for allowing me to teach Snap using their remote classroom infrastructure.

Finally, this book would not have been possible without the constant encouragement of my friends and family.

I do hope that you will find this book useful and enjoyable.

Abhay B. Joshi (abjoshi@yahoo.com)
Seattle, USA
5 October 2020

Author's Background

As a freelance teacher (since 2008), Abhay's area of interest has been "teaching Computer Programming as a medium for learning" and he has been teaching Snap, Python, and Scratch regularly to middle and high school students – currently in the Pacific Northwest of USA and Pune, India.

Since 2011 Abhay has authored several books for a series aimed at *Learning computer programming and CS principles*. He now has a set of 4 books on Scratch Programming which anyone can use to start from the basics and become an expert Scratch programmer. He has also written books on Logo Programing – the granddaddy of and inspiration behind most modern languages meant for CS education. Abhay has written several articles to promote CS education, and has conducted teacher-training workshops to encourage aspiring teachers to experiment with this idea.

Abhay has been associated with the Software Industry since 1988 as a programmer, developer, entrepreneur, coach, and adviser. After getting an MS in Computer Engineering from Syracuse University (USA), he worked as a programmer for product companies that developed operating systems, network protocols, and secure software. In 1997, Abhay co-founded Disha Technologies, a successful software services organization.

Programming remains one of Abhay's favorite hobbies, and he continues to explore the "entertaining, intellectual, and educational" aspects of programming.

Author's CS page: http://www.abhayjoshi.net/spark/home.htm

Table of Contents

Every computer program is a model, hatched in the mind, of a real or mental process. These processes, arising from human experience and thought, are huge in number, intricate in detail, and at any time only partially understood.

- Alan J. Perlis

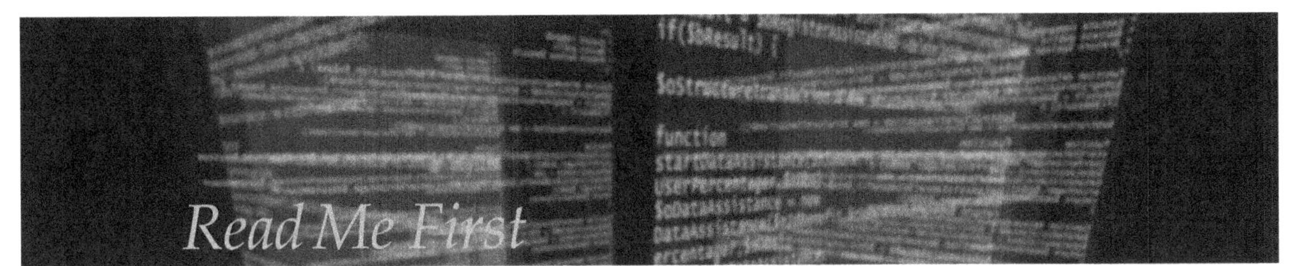

Design Process

This book is organized as a series of independent Snap projects – each of which describes how to design and build an interesting and challenging Snap program. Every project follows a certain common design methodology. The purpose of this chapter is to get you familiarized with this methodology, so that you will then be able to explore any project without difficulty.

Divide and conquer technique

We build each program *incrementally*, i.e. we use a methodology called "Divide and Conquer". Let us see an example to understand how to go about using this technique.

In the "divide and conquer" approach, we take a step back and think about (or if available take a careful look at) our final outcome and ask the question, *"What is this program made up of? Can we break it up into separate parts that are meaningful and possibly reusable?"*

Once we identify such components of the program, we go about designing each of them separately.

In other words, we call our complete program as the "Big Idea" and break it down into smaller *feature ideas*. We list these various feature ideas in what is called the "high level design".

For example, if we wanted to design the house shown below, we would first take a step back and take a keen look at the house and ask the question: "What is this house made up of? Can we break it apart into meaningful reusable components or parts?"

We come up with the answer: "Yes, we see three parts: a wall, a roof, and a window."

Then, it is a matter of designing each of these components (*wall* which is a square, *roof* which is a sitting triangle, and *window* which is a 2x2 pattern of squares) separately and putting them together to get a house.

There are several advantages of using this "divide and conquer" methodology, some of which are listed below:

1. It simplifies our overall task considerably. In the *house* program, designing a square, a triangle, etc. is simpler than designing the entire house at once. It is also much easier to go back and correct problems in these smaller components.
2. The components can be reused. In the *house* program, the square design used for the wall can be reused in the window design.
3. The final program becomes much more flexible. In the *house* program, by drawing walls, roofs, and windows of different sizes we can draw houses of different kind and size.

How do we identify the smaller feature ideas in our Snap programs? We do that first by playing with the actual running program (whose link is provided at the end of every chapter). Then we take a keen look at the main screen of the program and try to identify its different pieces, such as, sprites, the function of each of them, and how they interact. We list these feature ideas in a section called the "High Level Design".

Incremental design

The next step is to actually design these various feature ideas one by one. This design process is generally stated as below:

1. Take a smaller feature idea (a part of the "big idea").
2. Think about how it can be implemented (experiment in Snap if necessary).
3. Write the scripts.
4. Test and verify that the scripts work as expected. If not, repeat steps 2, 3, and 4 until the idea works as expected.
5. Repeat from step 1 (take up another smaller feature idea). Continue until all required features have been added to the program.

Object Oriented Thinking

You might have heard terms such as "Object oriented design" or "Object oriented programming". These are advanced program design ideas – typically taught in college-level courses, but they are all basically based on a simpler idea called object oriented thinking. An example may work best to understand this idea.

Let's say we want to write a "circus" interactive animation program in which different actors (humans and animals) perform various acts of acrobatics. They perform these acts only when requested by the user. We could think of every actor as an "object" in our program with the following attributes:

- Its own data variables that describe its properties if any. For example, a tiger may have a "color" property which could be yellow or white.
- Its own scripts (procedures) that implement its actions. For example, a tiger may have a script called "Jump thru a ring of fire" which would show the tiger jumping thru a ring of fire.
- Means to accept commands from the user or other objects. These means may include click buttons or broadcast messages.
- Means to communicate with other objects if required. These means may be broadcast messages or variables. For example, our tiger may have an act that requires it to coordinate its "jumping thru a ring of fire" while an elephant is performing some other act.

In this book, I have tried to introduce this type of thinking wherever possible.

Flow of Each Chapter

As already mentioned, the book consists of a series of independent Snap projects. Every chapter follows a certain common flow and structure. I will now get you familiarized with this structure, so that you will then be able to pick any project and go through its flow with ease.

All project chapters contain the same sections as listed (and explained) below.

Program Description

In this section we describe how the final program is used by its users. If it's a game, we will describe the rules of the game; if it's an interactive animation we will describe what the animation does, and so on.

I will then provide a link to a working Snap version of the program which you should check out. I encourage you to explore the program and its various features before reading the chapter further. But, be sure not to look at the Snap scripts of the program, because we want to design them ourselves.

Snap and CS Concepts Used

This section lists the Snap and CS concepts that you will need to know when you design this program. I assume that you are already familiar with these concepts.

High Level Design

This is where we list the multiple smaller ideas which can be programmed separately. Using the "divide and conquer" technique, we study the main screen of the program and try to come up with this list of feature ideas.

Program Versions

A "program version" is nothing but a copy of your Snap project with a unique name. In the process of designing our Snap program step by step, we will develop multiple program versions, such as, project-1, project-2, etc. Each version will include a subset of the feature ideas. As the version number increases, it indicates that the program has more and more features.

Project 1: Tic-Tac-Toe

Program description

Tic-tac-toe is a paper-and-pencil game for two players, X and O, who take turns marking the spaces in a 3×3 grid. The player who succeeds in placing three of their marks in a horizontal, vertical, or diagonal row is the winner.

The above picture shows a finished round in which O won.

If you are unfamiliar with the rules of this game, look up:
https://en.wikipedia.org/wiki/Tic-tac-toe

Our Snap program will allow the user to play against the computer.

Explore the game:

If you want to play with my final program to get a feel for this game, open the link given at the end of the chapter. Try not to peek at the scripts yet, since we want to design them ourselves below.

1. Click the "Green flag".
2. Follow the instructions.
3. In the first round, the player (you) get to play first. In subsequent rounds, the program decides randomly who will go first.

Snap and CS Concepts Used

When we design this program, we will make use of the following Snap and CS concepts. Learn these concepts if you don't know them before proceeding further.

- Algorithms
    - Designing new algorithms
- Arithmetic
    - Expressions
    - Basic operators (+, -, x, /)
- Backdrops – multiple
- Concurrency
    - Synchronization using broadcasting
- Conditional statements:
    - Conditions: YES/NO questions
    - Relational operators (=, <, >)
    - Conditionals (IF)
    - Conditionals (If-Else)
    - Conditionals (nested IF)
    - Boolean operators (and, or, not)
- Data structures – list
    - List operations
    - Using list as 2-D array
- Data types – basic
    - Integers
- Data types – strings

- o   String operations (join, letter, length of)
- Events
- Looping (iteration)
  - o   Looping - simple (repeat, forever)
  - o   Looping - nested
  - o   Looping - conditional (repeat until)
- OOP
  - o   Clones
  - o   Clones differentiation: using private id
- Procedures
  - o   User defined (custom)
  - o   Procedures with parameters and return value
- Program output
  - o   Text
- Random numbers
- Sequence
- Stopping scripts
- User input
  - o   Text
  - o   Click buttons
- Variables
  - o   Simple
  - o   Local/global scope
  - o   Script-local
- XY Geometry

Version 1 High Level Design

This "dumb" version of our program only supplies the logistics of the game, i.e. the board, and allows 2 human players play the game between them.

Let's consider how the various features of this program can be separated out as distinct pieces.

This is how the initial screen looks like in my program:

Tic-tac-toe

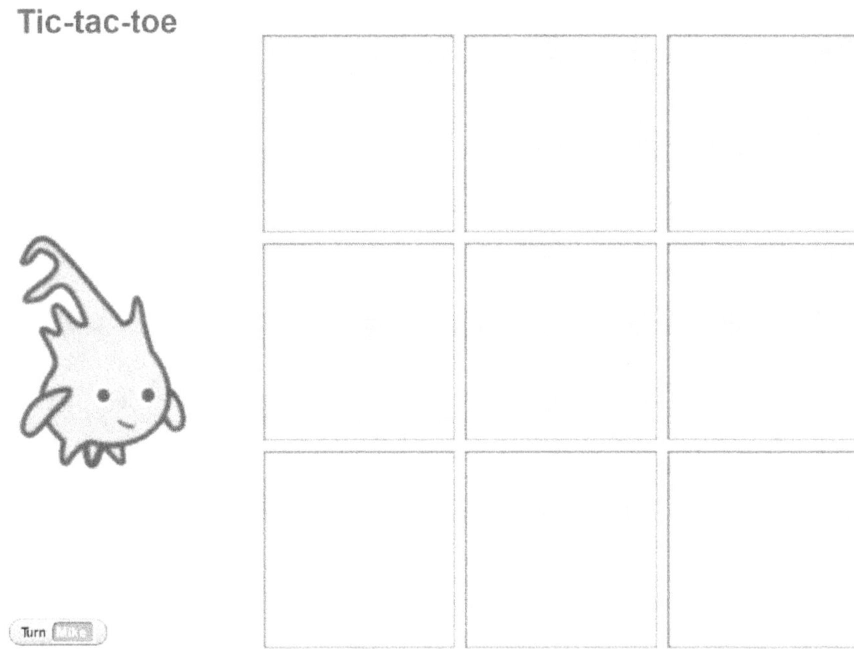

As usual, we can consider the backend and the frontend separately. The backend will hold the board in some variable(s) and will have all the logic to manipulate the contents of the board as the game proceeds. The frontend will display the board in a 3x3 grid format and pass user input (which cell was clicked) to the backend. The frontend will always show the current state of the board.

For the frontend, I will borrow an older program called "matrix" from the book "Practice CS Concepts with Snap" which provides just this functionality using clones. (Note: The matrix program is available in the files provided with this book. Refer to the book's introduction.)

The backend will internally represent the board as a 9-item list. The backend logic needs to do the following:
  (1) Keep track of the 2 players: let's call them Fred and Prem. Fred will use the Xs and Prem the Os.
  (2) Keep track of whose turn it is. We can do this by using a variable that alternates between the two players.

(3) Whenever a blank cell is clicked, fill it with the current player's shape.

(4) Detect when the game is over and declare the winner. For this purpose, we will need an algorithm (procedure) to scan the entire board for a row, column, or diagonal filled with the same shape (X or O).

Objects:

We will distribute the code among the following objects:

- Frontend "Square" sprite will contain all logic related to the visible 3x3 grid.
- Backend logic will contain all code related to features described above.
- Stage will do some coordination.

Feature Idea # 1: The tic-tac-toe board

Draw a 3x3 grid of clickable cells.

Design:

Step 1: The visible board

As mentioned earlier, we will start with an older program called "matrix" which provides just this functionality using clones. This includes a "square" sprite that displays a 3x3 grid using clones.

Each clone will possess a unique id so that the backend can associate each visible cell with a location on the game board. When a cell is clicked, this unique id will be sent to the backend via a variable.

Step 2: The board state

As discussed earlier, we will use a 9-item list to represent the 3x3 board. The 9-item list would be one dimensional whereas the board is 2-D. How does each cell associate itself with an item in the list? Well, each clone will have a unique "id" (as mentioned already) that will number the cells 1 thru 9 as they are created and laid out from top to bottom. Thus, the first row of cells would be items 1 thru 3 in the list, and so on.

When a cell is clicked, it can simply refer to its "id" to know which item in the list it belongs to and set it to X or O. For a reason that will become clear soon, we will use numbers to represent the shapes: 1 for X, -1 for O, and 0 for blank. When a cell is clicked, its state will be changed based on whose turn it is. And to ensure the visible board is in sync, the backend will send a "refresh" message every time the board state changes.

Feature Idea # 2: Show the Xs and the Os

When a player clicks on a blank cell his/her shape (X or O) is placed.

Design:

We will use a "player" variable to keep track of whose turn it is. Fred plays first and uses the Xs. Prem plays second and uses the Os. In order to display the shapes, we could allow each "square" to have 3 costumes: one blank, one with X and one with O. Depending on the state of each cell (controlled by the backend), the appropriate costume can be turned up. The "refresh" script in frontend will synchronize the display with the state of the actual board.

Feature Idea # 3: Winner

After every move check the board for a winner.

Design:

This is the most challenging part so far. We need to scan rows, columns, and diagonals to detect a winner. This is where our earlier decision to denote an X with 1 and an O with -1 comes handy.

To check if a row, column, or diagonal is filled with the same shape, we can simply add up the numbers. If the sum is 3, Fred is the winner. If the sum is -3, Prem is the winner. All other cases do not matter.

Now, let's design the algorithms for the scanning task. While we are at it, we should also check the condition when the grid becomes full (see the last algorithm).

 | *Adventures in Snap Programming*

Algorithm for scanning rows:

There are 3 rows starting at item 1, 4, and 7 respectively. Each row consists of 3 consecutive items. Using this information we can come up with the algorithm as below:

```
I = 1
Repeat 3 times
     Add up items I, I+1, and I+2
     If sum is 3, Fred is the winner
     If sum is -3, Prem is the winner
     I = I + 3
End repeat
```

Algorithm for scanning columns:

There are 3 columns starting at item 1, 2, and 3 respectively. Each column consists of 3 items 3 places apart of each other. For example, the first column consists of items 1, 4, and 7. The second column consists of items 2, 5, and 8. And so on. Using this information we can come up with the algorithm as below:

```
I = 1
Repeat 3 times
     Add up items I, I+3, and I+6
     If sum is 3, Fred is the winner
     If sum is -3, Prem is the winner
     I = I + 1
End repeat
```

Algorithm for scanning diagonals:

There are 2 diagonals: one consists of items 1, 5, and 9, and the other consists of 3, 5, and 7. Here is the algorithm:

```
Add up items 1, 5, and 9
     If sum is 3, Fred is the winner
     If sum is -3, Prem is the winner
Add up items 3, 5, and 7
     If sum is 3, Fred is the winner
     If sum is -3, Prem is the winner
```

Algorithm for grid full condition:

This is a simple algorithm in which we just need to check if there isn't a single item which is 0.

```
I = 1
Repeat 9
      If I'th element is 0
            Return false
      End if
      Increment I by 1
End repeat
Return true
```

Save as Program Version 1

Congratulations! You have completed all the features of Version 1. Compare your program with my program in the file below.

File: tic-tac-toe-1.xml

Version 2 High Level Design

In this "intelligent" version, we will allow the computer to be one of the players. The computer won't really use any intelligence for the moves, but will pick moves randomly from the available blank cells.

Most of the logic of Version 1 can be used as is. In order to allow the computer to play, we will need to "simulate" a click, i.e. be able to run the "when cell clicked" script when the computer picks a cell. And then, the computer will play in place of "Prem". "Simulation" basically means causing a click from inside the program.

Feature Idea # 4: Simulate click

Arrange the code such that a cell can be clicked from inside the program.

Design:

Right now, the "when this sprite clicked" script for the clones doesn't do any work; it just sends the clone's id to the backend. So, the "computer" player can do the same, i.e. when it is its turn to play, it can pick its cell and message its id to the backend.

Feature Idea # 5: Replace Prem by Computer

Have the computer play in place of Prem.

Design:

Right now, whenever it is Prem's turn to play, the program just waits for him to click. Instead, the program will "simulate" a click by sending a broadcast message (as made possible by Feature idea #4 above).

Step 1: Send a broadcast message when it is Prem's turn.

At the end of the "click processing" script we can check the "player" variable and if it is "Prem" – indicating that it is Prem's turn – we can initiate the broadcast message.

Step 2: Pick a blank cell at random.

Of course, before sending the broadcast message the computer needs to pick a cell at random from the available empty cells. The list L can tell us which cells are empty. We could count the empty cells and then use the pick random operator to pick one of them. See the algorithm below:

```
Count = number of empty cells (items in L that are 0)
R = pick a random number between 1 and Count
The R'th empty cell is our cell.
```

The nice thing about algorithms is there can be multiple approaches to solve the same problem. For example, here is another approach to select a random empty cell:

```
L = list of empty cells (items in L that are 0)
C = pick a random cell from L (Snap has a special command for this)
```

Save as Program Version 2

Congratulations! You have completed all the features of Version 2. Compare your program with my program in the file below.

File: tic-tac-toe-2.xml

Final version High Level Design

In this version, we will make the computer a bit more intelligent. We will use some simple rules to avoid completely dumb moves. For example, if the opponent is about to win (when only one blank cell is remaining to complete a row, column, or diagonal), the computer should thwart that possibility. Conversely, if the computer sees an opportunity to win (when a row, column, or diagonal is already filled with 2 of its own shapes) it should grab it. Since the basic work for both these rules is the same, we can combine it in a single feature idea as explained below.

Feature Idea # 6: Fill the 3rd cell

Check if the 3rd cell of a row, column, or diagonal helps you win or prevent a loss.

Design:

We will once again have to scan all rows, columns, and diagonals and check for this state. The above algorithms (used in Feature #3 for scanning) can be adapted for this purpose. We should first look for "win" before worrying about "loss", right? This can cause duplication of work, because we will need to scan all rows (or columns or diagonals) for "win" and then scan again for a "loss". One workaround to avoid this duplication is to give priority to a win, but remember a "lossy" row. See the algorithms below to understand this better.

Algorithm for scanning rows:
There are 3 rows starting at item 1, 4, and 7 respectively. Each row consists of 3 consecutive items. Using this information we can come up with the algorithm as below:

```
Algorithm: ScanRowsForWinLoss
Return value: cell index to use or 0
I = 1
retVal = 0
Repeat 3 times
      Add up items I, I+1, and I+2
      If sum is 2 or -2
            Locate the empty cell and save its index in J
      End if
      retVal = J
      If sum is -2  // chance to win!
```

```
        Return retVal
    End if
    // do nothing if sum is 2
    I = I + 3  // go to the next row
End repeat
Return retVal // opportunity to avoid loss
```

Algorithm for scanning columns:

There are 3 columns starting at item 1, 2, and 3 respectively. Each column consists of 3 items 3 places apart of each other. For example, the first column consists of items 1, 4, and 7. The second column consists of items 2, 5, and 8. And so on. Using this information we can come up with the algorithm as below:

```
Algorithm: ScanColumnsForWinLoss
Return value: cell index to use or 0
I = 1
retVal = 0
Repeat 3 times
        Add up items in this column (items I, I+3, and I+6)
        If sum is 2 or -2
                Locate the empty cell and save its index in J
        End if
        retVal = J
        If sum is -2  // chance to win!
                Return retVal
        End if
        // do nothing if sum is 2
        I = I + 1  // go to the next column
End repeat
Return retVal // opportunity to avoid loss
```

Algorithm for scanning diagonals:

There are 2 diagonals: one consists of items 1, 5, and 9, and the other consists of 3, 5, and 7. Here is the algorithm:

```
Algorithm: ScanDiagonalsForWinLoss
Return value: cell index to use or 0
retVal = 0
Add up items 1, 5, and 9
        If sum is 2 or -2
                Locate the empty cell and save its index in J
        End if
        retVal = J
```

```
      If sum is -2  // chance to win!
            Return retVal
      End if
      // do nothing if sum is 2
Add up items 3, 5, and 7
      If sum is 2 or -2
            Locate the empty cell and save its index in J
      End if
      retVal = J
      If sum is -2  // chance to win!
            Return retVal
      End if
      // do nothing if sum is 2
Return retVal // opportunity to avoid loss
```

Save as Program Version "Final"

Congratulations! You have completed all the main features of the Tic-tac-toe game. Compare your program with my program in the file below.

File: Tic-tac-toe-final.xml

Also published on the Berkeley Snap website: Tic-Tac-Toe
(https://snap.berkeley.edu/snapsource/snap.html#present:Username=abjoshi&ProjectName=tic-tac-toe-final)

How to play the game:

1. Click the "Green flag".
2. Follow the instructions.
3. In the first round, the player (you) get to play first. In subsequent rounds, the program decides randomly who will go first.

Project 2: Connect Four

"Play" doesn't require open spaces or expensive toys; it requires a combination of curiosity, imagination, and experimentation.
– Mitchel Resnick

Program description

Connect Four is a 2-player game which consists of two sets of colored coins and a standing grid of rows and columns. Each player takes one set of coins and then by turn drops coins down any of the vertical columns (we will call them "tubes"). See the picture below.

The goal of the game is to get 4 coins of the same color to arrange themselves along a row, column, or diagonal. The first player to do this wins the game.

If you want to play with my final program to get a feel for this game, open the link mentioned at the end of the chapter. Try not to peek at the scripts yet, since we want to design them ourselves below.

How to run the program:
1. Click the "Green flag" to start the game. Press "h" to view help.
2. You (the human player) begin with an "Orange" coin and the computer plays with "Blue" coins. The variable "Turn" shows whose turn it is.
3. Set the slider variable "Monkey coins" to determine how many coins the computer will get to drop at every turn.
4. Click the base of the tube in which you want to drop your coin.

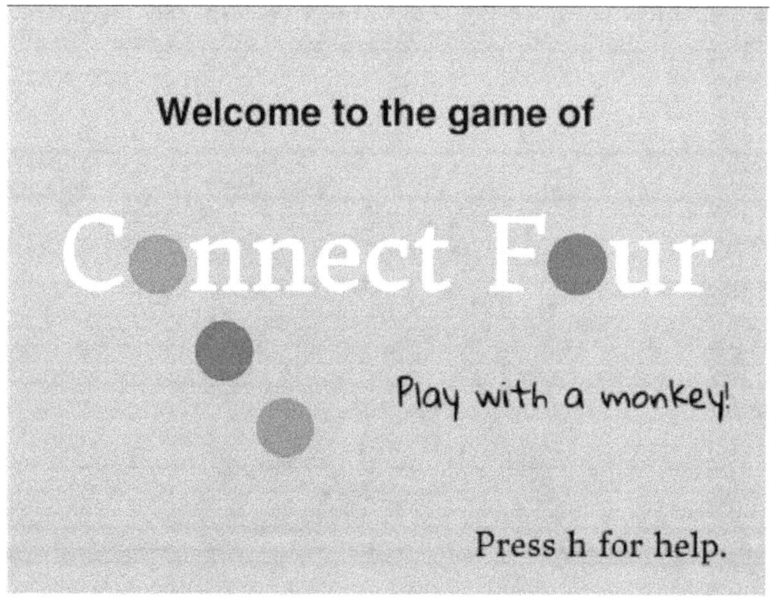

Snap and CS Concepts Used

When we design this program, we will make use of the following Snap and CS concepts. Learn these concepts if you don't know them before proceeding further.

- Algorithms
    - o Abstraction
    - o Using algorithms
    - o Designing new algorithms
    - o Pseudo-code
- Arithmetic
    - o Expressions
    - o Basic operators (+, -, x, /)
- Backdrops – multiple
- Concurrency
    - o Synchronization using broadcasting
- Conditional statements:
    - o Conditions: YES/NO questions
    - o Relational operators (=, <, >)
    - o Conditionals (IF)
    - o Conditionals (If-Else)
    - o Conditionals (Wait until)
    - o Conditionals (nested IF)
    - o Boolean operators (and, or, not)
- Data structures – list
    - o List operations
    - o Using list as 2-D array
    - o List traversal
- Data types – strings
    - o String operations (join, letter, length of)
- Events
- Geometry - parallel lines
- Looping (iteration)
    - o Looping - simple (repeat, forever)
    - o Looping – simple, with counter (for)

-      o   Looping - conditional (repeat until)
- Motion
    - o   Motion - absolute
    - o   Motion - smooth using repeat
- OOP
    - o   Clones
    - o   Clones differentiation: using private id
- Pen commands
- Procedures
    - o   Built-in
    - o   User defined (custom)
    - o   With inputs
    - o   With return value
- Program output
    - o   Text
- Sequence
- Sounds - playing sounds
- User input
    - o   Click buttons
- Variables
    - o   Simple
    - o   Properties (built-in)
    - o   Local/global scope
- XY Geometry

High Level Design:

This is where we take a step away from the computer, analyze the problem in our mind (and on a piece of paper if necessary), and break it down into multiple smaller ideas which can be programmed separately.

Let's take a look at the main screen of the game and try to point out the different pieces.

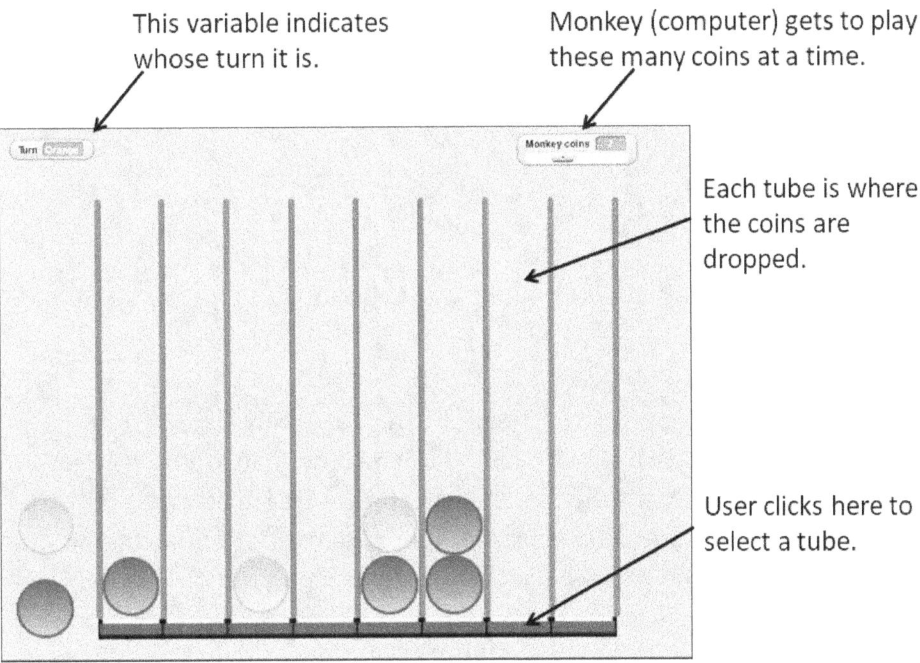

Initial Set of Features:

Clearly it makes sense to start with the most basic apparatus – which is 2 sets of coins and the grid. At this stage, we *won't* trouble ourselves with the actual playing part or rules of the game (as listed in "program description" above). We will implement the game's main user interface and get all sprites in place. How will we represent the collection of coins? Once a coin is dropped in a tube, it doesn't do anything. So, we could use just 2 coin sprites and use their clones to create the dropped coins. We also need a grid of identical tubes (columns) each with a solid clickable base.

That will be our starting version of the game. We will discuss what to do next after building this version.

Let us get rolling with these various ideas one by one.

Feature Idea # 1: Coins and the grid

Draw the coin sprites and the grid of vertical tubes.

Step 1: Draw the coin sprites.

Design:

To play the game we need lots of orange and lots of blue coins. But, how many *sprites* do we need?

Let us consider what happens to each coin. When a coin is dropped into a tube it just sits there until the game is over. We can use the clone feature to create an image of a coin when it is dropped in a tube. So, that means we just need two sprites: one for the orange coin and one for the blue coin. We will take care of the actual script later. For now, we will just draw the sprites.

Draw circle sprites with thick border. Fill them with gradient of the same color. Resize them such that they fit the width of the tube.

Step 2: Draw the grid (series of tubes).

Design:

It is really up to us to decide how many tubes we should have. In my program, I have drawn 8 tubes. You can do the same or use a different number.

The grid, as you can see, has two parts:
1.   A series of vertical lines which define the tubes
2.   A solid base for each tube

The solid base of each tube will have to be a separate sprite, because, the players will select a tube by clicking its base. We can just draw one base and create duplicate sprites.

The vertical lines can be drawn as a sprite (or part of the background), but it is quite tedious to draw equidistant (equally spaced) parallel lines in the paint editor. Instead, we will draw them in the program itself using the Pen commands and some simple geometry.

First, we will draw the 8 bottom sprites and line them up in a straight line near the bottom of the screen. Next, we will draw the tubes above them.

The algorithm to draw the lines for the tubes is quite simple. Let's say "w" is the width and "h" is the height of each tube. Let's say point (x, y) is on the left edge of the first base.

Algorithm to draw the tubes:

```
Go to x, y
Repeat 9
       Pen down
       Change y by h
       Pen up
       Change y by -h
       Change x by w
End repeat
```

Save as Program Version 1

Before continuing to the next set of ideas, we will save our project. This way, we have a backup of our project that we can go back to if required for any reason.

Next Set of Features/ideas:

Next, we will write scripts for dropping coins in the tubes. This involves the following features:

- Choosing a tube
- Choosing the right coin to drop
- Positioning a coin on top of the selected tube
- Dropping a coin down the selected tube
- When a tube becomes full, don't allow coins to drop in it.

Let us get cracking with these ideas and features one by one.

Feature Idea # 2: Choosing tube and coin

Implement a way for the players to choose a tube, and have a way for the players to take turns.

Design:

Selecting a tube is straightforward. Since each tube has a separate base sprite, the players can simply click on the base to choose a tube.

To ensure players play by turn, we can have a variable called "Turn" which will indicate whose turn it is. If it says "Orange" an orange coin will be dropped and if it says "Blue" a blue coin will be dropped.

Feature Idea # 3: Drop the coin

Write scripts to position the selected coin on top of the selected tube and drop it into the selected tube.

Step 1: Position the coin on top of the selected tube.

Design:

The variable "Turn" tells us which coin is to be dropped. The player will click on the base of the selected tube. In order to position a coin on top of this tube we need to know the X and Y co-ordinates of the point. We can pick some arbitrary value of Y which is somewhere above all tubes. This value would work for all tubes since they are all of the same height. How about X?

Well, we can use the X of the base sprite, right? Each base, when clicked, can save its X position in a global variable.

There is one last thing we need to take care of. Since clones inherit everything of their parents, including its scripts, the "fall" script will be run by the parents as well as all clones. We need to prevent this and ensure only the parents run this script.

There is one way: we will use a private variable called "my id" whose value would be different for the parents and for each clone. And then, the "fall" script will check this id (and ensure it matched the parent's) before proceeding.

Step 2: Drop the coin into the selected tube.

Design:
Making the coin fall into the tube is straightforward. We can make it move downward until it reaches the top coin in the tube (or the tube's bottom if it's empty).

The coin sprite will create a clone which will perform the actual motion of falling down the tube. The clone needs to know the starting and ending (x, y) for its motion. We calculated the X and Y of the starting point above. What about the ending point? Well, the X value will clearly be the same. If we knew the number of existing coins in the tube and the coin's diameter, we can calculate the ending Y point also.

Y = Y of the 1st coin + (diameter of each coin) x number of coins in the tube

We will maintain an 8-item list called "coins in tubes" in which each item will tell us how many coins there are in that tube. For example, item 1 will tell # of coins in the 1st tube, item 2 will tell # of coins in the 2nd tube, and so on.

But, who will create and maintain this list? Well, every time a coin is dropped in a tube we will increment its corresponding count in this list.

Feature Idea # 4: Tube full condition
When a tube becomes full, don't allow coins to drop in it.

Design:

There are different ways to implement this feature. For example, you could keep a count of the number of coins inside each tube in a list variable, and check that count every time a coin is dropped.

If you remember, we already have a list called "coins in tubes" that tells us how many coins each tube has any time. We can just refer to this list each time before calling the "fall" script. The "click" script of each tube sprite (i.e. the base sprite) will thus look as follows:

```
When sprite clicked:
If # of coins in my tube is less than 7
      Set X and Y of starting point
      Call "fall" script (send broadcast)
End if
```

Save as Program Version 2

Before continuing to the next set of ideas, we will save our project. This way, we have a backup of our project that we can go back to if required for any reason.

How to run the program:

1. Click the "Green flag" to start the game.
2. Two users (blue and orange) will play the game by clicking alternately. The variable "Turn" shows whose turn it is.
3. Click the base of the tube in which you want to drop your coin.

Final Set of Features/ideas:

We need to implement one important feature of the game: determining the winner. We will also add a few more features to make the program more tidy, robust, and user-friendly. Here are the things we will consider in this version:

-   Add a welcome screen, help screen and sounds.
-   Add code that will automatically place the pipe bases in a neat row.
-   Detect winner.

- Detect stalemate (i.e. board becoming full).

Let us get cracking with these ideas and features one by one.

Feature Idea # 5: Welcome and Help Screens

Add a welcome screen, a help screen and suitable sounds.

Design:

This should be a straightforward task. We will arrange the code such that the welcome screen appears when Green Flag is clicked and everything else is hidden at that time. After a short time (say 4 seconds) the game screen will appear.

The help screen will be optional – available when some key is pressed. It should go away when the mouse pointer is clicked anywhere.

What about sounds? Well, I have added one sound clip which plays every time a coin is dropped.

Feature Idea # 6: Placement of bases

Use a script to automatically place the bases in a neat row.

Design:

This is a matter of using the X-Y geometry and the "Go to x, y" command. Since all bases are at the same height, the Y position of all will be the same. Now, if you know the width of each base and the x position of the first base, can you calculate the x positions of the subsequent bases?

Here is the algorithm for these calculations:

```
Let x be the position of the first base
Let w be the width of each base
X position of the 2nd base = x + 1*w
X position of the 3rd base = x + 2*w
X position of the 4th base = x + 3*w
And so on …
```

Do you get the idea? Since sprites only move by themselves (and others cannot move them), each base can run this code to place itself under "when green flag clicked".

Feature Idea # 7: Determine the winner
The program should detect and declare winner when 4 coins of either color line up contiguously vertically, horizontally, or diagonally.

Design:
This is the most challenging feature thus far! For this, we first need to find a way for the program to see the entire board of 8 tubes that can each hold 7 coins max. Basically we will need some data structure that can internally represent the "7 rows x 8 columns" matrix of the Connect 4 board.

We could use a list of lists to represent a 2 dimensional matrix. For example, the first item in this list would represent the 1st row, the next item would represent the 2nd row, and so on. (Note: We could have made each item represent a tube also, but just to conform to the convention of "rows of columns" we give priority to the rows.)

Data structure:
A list variable called "grid": this will consist of 7 sub-lists with each sub-list in turn containing 8 items. This grid represents the 56 cells of Connect 4 board initially all set to 0.

Rows will be counted bottom-up (i.e. 1st sub-list is the *bottom* row of Connect 4), and columns will be counted left to right as usual.

Every time a coin is dropped in, we will record its presence in this grid: we would know its "column" simply from which tube was clicked, and its "row" from the "coins in tube" list. We will record the coin by using its color: "orange" or "blue".

Let us now design the algorithms to detect a winner.

This is the approach we will use: every time a coin is dropped, it will occupy a cell C in "grid". We will then scan cells adjacent to C horizontally, vertically, and diagonally to check if there are 4 contiguous cells with the same color as C. Since we will run this algorithm every time a coin is dropped, we don't need to scan the entire grid, but just the area adjacent to this coin.

Do you get the idea? The following example might help:

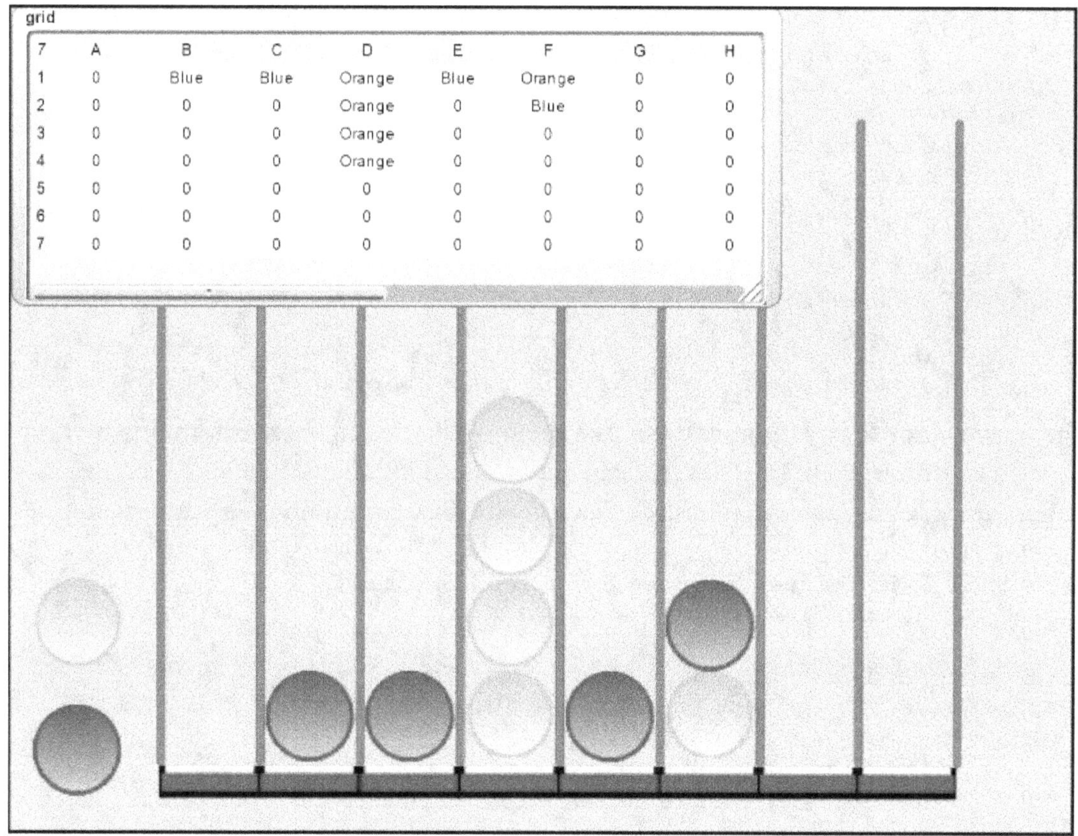

In this image, we see a snapshot of the Connect 4 program. The "grid" list is shown in table format (Snap allows you to view a list of lists in this format). The last coin dropped was the orange coin in tube 4. The algorithm will scan cells in its vicinity and discover that there are indeed 4 orange coins lined up contiguously in column 4, and hence it will go ahead and return "True" (i.e. a winner was found).

Here is the algorithm:

```
Algorithm "Is There a Winner"
(Called when a coin is dropped)
Input: row, column, color
For the row:
     Count left and right from current position, if 4 contiguous
     coins of 'color' found return True
For the column:
     Count up and down from current position, if 4 contiguous coins
     of 'color' found return True
For diagonals:
     Count NW and SE from current position, if 4 contiguous coins of
     'color' found return True
     Count NE and SW from current position, if 4 contiguous coins of
     'color' found return True
No contiguous pattern found, so return False
```

The above algorithm, as you can see, is just an outline of all the work that is involved. Let's now enumerate the details of each step of scanning. Note that since the input cell (whose row, col are passed) is counted twice, our final condition is "count > 4"

```
Algorithm Check Winner in Rows( row, col, color )
In the given "row":
Count = 0
Scan cells to the right (by incrementing "col")
Stop scanning if (1) end of board is reached or (2) if the cell
contains a different color coin
        - Increment Count for each cell
Scan cells to the left (by decrementing "col")
Stop scanning if (1) end of board is reached or (2) if the cell
contains a different color coin
        - Increment Count for each cell
If Count > 4 return true
Else return false
```

Algorithm Check Winner in Columns(row, column, color)
In the given "column":
Count = 0
Scan cells up (by incrementing "row")
Stop scanning if (1) end of board is reached or (2) if the cell
contains a different color coin
        - Increment Count for each cell
Scan cells down (by decrementing "row")
Stop scanning if (1) end of board is reached or (2) if the cell
contains a different color coin
        - Increment Count for each cell
If count > 4 return true
Else return false

Algorithm Check Winner in NE-SW diagonal (row, col, color)
Count = 0
Scan cells in NE direction (by incrementing both "row" and "col")
Stop scanning if (1) end of board is reached or (2) if the cell
contains a different color coin
        - Increment Count for each cell
Scan cells in SW direction (by decrementing both "row" and "col")
Stop scanning if (1) end of board is reached or (2) if the cell
contains a different color coin
        - Increment Count for each cell
If count > 4 return True
Else return False

Algorithm Check Winner in NW-SE diagonal (row, col, color)
Count = 0
Scan cells in NW direction (by incrementing "row" and decrementing
"col")
Stop scanning if (1) end of board is reached or (2) if the cell
contains a different color coin
        - Increment Count for each cell
Scan cells in SE direction (by incrementing "col" and decrementing
"row")
Stop scanning if (1) end of board is reached or (2) if the cell
contains a different color coin
        - Increment Count for each cell
If count > 4 return True
Else return False

Feature Idea # 8: Detect stalemate

The program should detect when the entire board becomes full without anyone winning.

Design:

Now that we have the "grid" data structure that continuously shows the state of the Connect 4 board, we can easily detect when the grid becomes full of coins. Basically, we will need to scan the entire grid and look for empty cells, i.e. cells containing 0. See the algorithm below:

```
Algorithm "Is Grid Full"
For every row of grid
      For every column of grid
            If cell at (row, column) contains 0
                  Return False
            End if
      End for
End for
```

We will call this script after checking winner.

Save as the Final Program Version

Congratulations! You have completed the program with all the features we had planned. Save your program as "Connect4-final.xml".

Compare your program with my program below.

File: Connect4-final.xml

How to run the program:
1. Click the "Green flag" to start the game.
2. Two users (blue and orange) will play the game by clicking alternately. The variable "Turn" shows whose turn it is.
3. Click the base of the tube in which you want to drop your coin.
4. Play until one of the players wins.

Advanced version:

How about playing with the computer? Make the computer play as one of the players. There are several ways to do this: one can think of making the computer "intelligent" so that it plays like a human. But, for the sake of simplicity, we will make our program play like a "monkey" – with little or no intelligence. Even with that approach, as you will see, there are ways to make the computer a worthy, if not formidable, opponent.

Feature Idea # 9: Play with the computer

Make the program play as one of the players.

Step 1: Use the monkey algorithm for the computer player.

Design:

We will always start the game with the human player making the first move with the "Orange" coin. We will then have the program make the next move with the "Blue" coin. And so on.

"Making the move" for the computer would simply mean dropping the blue coin into one of the tubes. We already have the scripts that do all the work. We just need to "mimic" what happens when a user clicks on one of the tube bases, which is shown below:

```
When I am clicked:
If tube not full:
        tube = which tube
        tubex = my X position
        Ask my coin to fall
        Check if there is a winner
```

As mentioned above, we will use the "monkey" approach – which means the program will pick a tube at random. Once the tube has been decided, rest is a matter of duplicating the above actions. How will we get the tube's X position? Under "sensing" there is a reporter that gives you any property of any sprite.

Okay, so far so good. This monkey script would not really require a new sprite; we could give it to the stage. But how will it be invoked?

As mentioned above, this script should be invoked immediately after the human player has played. So, we could have the "When I am clicked" script above send a broadcast message – saying "hey monkey, it is your turn" – which would invoke the monkey script.

Here is the outline of the monkey script:

```
When "monkey turn" received:
Pick a tube "t" at random which is not full.
tube = t
tubex = X position of sprite "t"
Ask my coin to fall
Check if there is a winner
```

Step 2: Make the computer a "worthy" opponent.

Design:

You will notice that the monkey approach is quite disappointing because the human player can win almost every time with ease. How can we make the game a little more challenging?

Here is one idea. What if we allowed the computer to drop multiple coins at every turn? As it turns out, this can make the program a little more interesting because even if the coins are dropped randomly, with multiple blue coins there is less opportunity for the human player (who only gets to drop one coin) to win easily.

All we need to do then is use a "repeat" loop in the monkey script, and let the user set "how many" turns the computer should get. By default, we will set this variable to 2 and display it as a slider for the user to change.

There are a couple of small glitches that we need to fix. Currently the "Turn" variable determines whose turn it is, and this variable is switched after every coin drop. So the repeat loop in the "monkey script" will cause blue and orange coins to be dropped alternately!

This can be fixed easily by explicitly setting the "turn" variable to "Blue" in the monkey script.

The other glitch relates to the event when the game is over: either when someone wins or when the board becomes full. In these events, the monkey should stop playing because the game is over. But, the way we have written our program currently (see the "When I am clicked" script for each tube), the monkey script is called *after* checking these conditions, which means the monkey has no idea the game is over and will drop its coins regardless.

One easy fix is to call "stop all" when the game is over. That way, the monkey would have no opportunity to play its mischief.

Here is the final monkey script:

```
When "monkey turn" received:
Repeat "monkey coins" times:
      Find a tube "t" at random which is not full.
      Turn = Blue
      tube = t
      tubex = X position of sprite "t"
      Ask my coin to fall
      Check if there is a winner
```

Save as the Advanced Program Version

Congratulations! You have completed the program with all the advanced features we had planned. Save your program as "Connect4-advanced.xml".

Compare your program with my program below.

File: Connect4-advanced.xml

Link at Berkeley website: Connect4 advanced
`(https://snap.berkeley.edu/project?user=abjoshi&project=connect4-advanced)`

How to run the program:

1. Click the "Green flag" to start the game. Press "h" to view help.
2. You (the human player) begin with the "Orange" coin and the computer plays with "Blue" coins. The variable "Turn" shows whose turn it is.
3. Set the slider variable "Monkey coins" to determine how many coins the computer will get to drop at every turn.
4. Click the base of the tube in which you want to drop your coin.

Additional Challenge:

When a winner is detected, highlight the 4 balls that are lined up contiguously – either by changing their color or by making them blink.

Project 3: Eight Queen Puzzle

If you can't solve a problem, then there is an easier problem you can't solve: find it.
— George Polya

Program description

The eight queens puzzle is the problem of placing eight chess queens on an 8×8 chessboard so that no two queens threaten each other; thus, a solution requires that no two queens share the same row, column, or diagonal.

To learn more about this puzzle, look up the following page:
https://en.wikipedia.org/wiki/Eight_queens_puzzle

We will write a program that allows the user to solve this puzzle with the computer's help. The user can place queens themselves or can ask the computer any time to try to solve it further.

How the game is played:

- Take an empty chess board. Use the eight white (or black) pawns and assume that they are all queens.
- Place a queen anywhere on the board.
- Place another queen on the board such that it does not check the other queen.
- Continue placing the remaining queens in a similar fashion – none of them should check the rest.
- The challenge is thus to place all 8 queens on the board.

Here is an example:

Explore the game:

If you want to play with my final program to get a feel for this game, click the link given at the end of the chapter. Try not to peek at the scripts yet, since we want to design them ourselves below.

1. Click on the "Green flag": program begins with the instruction page. Click Continue to proceed.
2. The program will draw a new, empty chessboard.
3. In the 'manual' mode, you solve the puzzle. To place or remove a queen, simply click in a cell. The placement will be allowed only if there is no conflict with the existing queens on the board.
4. If you click the "Solve" button any time, the program attempts to solve the remaining puzzle. It doesn't change the current placement of queens that you have already made. If a solution is found, the program shows how long it took to solve. If no solution can be found, it says so.
5. Click "Restart" to go to step 2 above.

Snap and CS Concepts Used

When we design this program, we will make use of the following Snap and CS concepts. Learn these concepts if you don't know them before proceeding further.

- Algorithms
- Arithmetic
    - Expressions
    - Basic operators (+, -, x, /)
    - Advanced operators: mod, floor, etc.
- Concurrency
    - Synchronization using broadcasting
- Conditional statements:
    - Conditions: YES/NO questions
    - Relational operators (<, >, =)
    - Conditionals (IF)
    - Conditionals (If-Else)
    - Conditionals (nested IF)
    - Boolean operators (and, or, not)
- Data structures – list
    - List operations
    - Using list as 2-D array
- Data types – basic
    - Integers
- Data types – strings
    - String operations (join, split)
    - String traversal
- Events
- Looping (iteration)
    - Looping - simple (repeat, forever)
    - Looping – nested
    - Looping - conditional (repeat until)
- OOP
    - Clones
- Procedures
    - Built-in
    - User defined (custom)

o Simple
        o With inputs and return value
- Recursion
- Sequence
- User input
        o Click buttons
- Variables
        o Simple
        o Local/global scope
- XY Geometry

High Level Design

Let us consider how the various features of this program can be separated out as distinct pieces. As usual, we have the front-end that interacts with the user, and the back-end that performs all game functions.

Front-end components:
- 8x8 chess-board:
        o Keeps the display in sync with backend logic all the time
        o When the user clicks on a cell, informs the backend which cell was clicked
- 8 chess pieces (all queens)
        o If a cell contains a chess piece, its image is shown on top of the cell

For the frontend, we can simply borrow an older program called "chessboard" (from my earlier book "Practice CS Concepts with Snap") which provides just this functionality. Since all cells need to be click-sensitive, we will use "clones" to draw the board.

(Note: The chessboard program (chessboard.xml) is available in the files provided with this book. Refer to the Introduction section.)

Square sprite:
1. Draw the chessboard (using the clone feature). Each clone will save its cell id (1 thru 64) in its private variable.
2. Accept mouse clicks and identify the cell (row and column) in which the click happened. Send a message to the backend logic.
3. Keep display in sync with the contents of the backend board.

Queen sprite:
To display queen on the chessboard (using the clone feature). Each clone, if placed on the board, will save its row and column in its private variables.

Restart button sprite:
To accept a restart request from the user. It doesn't do any real work except sending a broadcast.

Solve button sprite:
To accept a "solve" request from the user. It doesn't do any real work except sending a broadcast.

Continue button sprite:
To accept a "continue" request from the user (on the help screen).

Conflict sprite:
To create the effect of a red light to indicate when a conflict of queens is detected in manual mode.

Back-end components:
- The initial layout is empty
- For every valid click (i.e. that satisfies game rules), the layout is modified.

Chessboard:
"Board" is 64-item list that will represent an 8x8 array of numbers, each representing a cell on the chessboard. Value of 1 means queen is present in that cell, 0 means the cell is empty.

Logic sprite:
All the logic algorithms (listed below) are implemented in this sprite.

Besides, it interfaces with the UI routines (of other sprites) through broadcast messages. For example: here is the logic when a cell is clicked: (a) Place or remove a queen on the board. (b) Allow placing only if there is no conflict. (c) Send "show queen" and "hide queen" to show or hide the queen sprite.

We will add methods (procedures/scripts) to these objects as we process each feature idea below.

We may also add more objects as we learn more about the features of the program.

Global data:

List "Board": 64 items, will hold the current status of the board, 0 for empty cell, 1 for the queen.
Integers "row" and "column": indicate the cell just clicked.

Feature Idea # 1: The chess board

Draw an 8x8 grid of chess-like cells.

Design:

As mentioned earlier, we will borrow an older program called "chessboard" and modify it to use clones instead of STAMP. Each square cell will have a private "cell id" (1 thru 64) using which we can calculate the row and column of the clicked cell using the following formulas.

```
Row = 1 + floor((Cell - 1) / 8)
Column = 1 + ((Cell - 1) mod 8)
```

Feature Idea # 2: Click cell

When a cell is clicked, place a queen if empty or remove it otherwise.

Design:

The user may click either on a square cell or on a queen. If the cell is empty a queen would be placed. If a conflict is detected, user is informed (by a flashing red light) and the queen is removed. If the cell already has a queen, it is removed. (Note: We will implement the "conflict check" in a later feature.)

Each square cell has a private "cell id" (1 thru 64) using which we can calculate the row and column of the clicked cell.

With the queen sprite (if it is clicked) it is much easier: each one has private variables row and column.

Upon calculating row and column of the clicked cell as above, the "flip cell" algorithm is invoked.

Flip cell
```
Input: row, column
If the cell is empty (no queen)
      Call PlaceQueen
      Call CheckConflict to check for conflict
            If true, show conflict and call RemoveQueen
Else call RemoveQueen
```

Place Queen
Place a queen at the given cell.
```
Input: row and column
Set the array location (row, column) to 1.
Display a queen at the cell: create clone of queen sprite at this
cell.
```

Remove Queen
Remove the queen at the given cell.
```
Input: row and column
Set the array location (row, column) to 0.
Send a message to queen sprite to hide: queen clone (with the right
row, column) will delete itself.
```


Feature Idea # 3: Check conflict
For the given cell (where a queen was just placed) check if it creates conflict on the board.

Design:
Simply stated, "conflict" would arise if two queens are in the same row, same column, or same diagonal. Before we confirm the placement of a new queen on the board, we need to ensure such conflict would not arise. Here is a list of algorithms that would take care of this requirement.

Check Conflict

Check conflict for the given cell. That is, with a queen placed at the current cell, check if the current row, current column, and current diagonals show conflict with other queens already on the board.

```
Given: row, column
Call CheckConflictRow to check if your row contains more than 1 queen.
Return if true.
Call CheckConflictColumn to check if your column contains more than 1
queen. Return if true.
Call CheckConflictDiagonalNW-SE to check if your NW-SE diagonal
contains more than 1 queen. Return if true.
Call CheckConflictDiagonalNE-SW to check if your NE-SW diagonal
contains more than 1 queen. Return if true.
```

CheckConflictRow

Check if the given row has more than 1 queen.
```
Input: row
Sum = 0
Add up 8 locations in "Board" starting from (row, 1)
If sum > 1
     There is conflict, return true
End if
```

CheckConflictColumn

Check if the given column has more than 1 queen.
```
Input: column
Sum = 0
Add up 8 row locations on "Board" starting from (1, column)
     (Hint: skip by 8 places)
If sum > 1
     There is conflict, return true
End if
```

CheckConflictDiagonalNE-SW

Check if the NE->SW diagonal contains more than 1 queen:
```
Input: row, col
Sum=0
Start from current cell: While both valid, decrement row and increment
column, and add to Sum each cell value.
Start from current cell: While both valid, increment row and decrement
column, and add to Sum each cell value.
Decrement Sum by current cell value because we counted it twice above.
```

```
If sum>1 return true.
Else return false.
```

CheckConflictDiagonalNW-SE

Check if the NW -> SE diagonal contains more than 1 queen:
```
Sum=0
Start from current cell: Until both valid, decrement row and decrement
column, and add to Sum each cell value.
Start from current cell: Until both valid, increment row and increment
column, and add to Sum each cell value.
Decrement Sum by current cell value because we counted it twice above.
If sum>1 return true.
Else return false.
```

Save as Program Version 1

Congratulations! You have completed all the basic features of the game. Compare your program with my program in the file below.

File: eight-queen-1.xml

How to play the game:
1. Click the "Green flag": program begins with the instruction page. Click Continue to proceed.
2. The program will draw a new, empty chessboard.
3. To place or remove a queen, simply click in a cell. The move will be allowed only if there is no conflict with the existing queens on the board.
4. Click "Restart" to go to step 2 above.

Feature Idea # 4: Auto mode

When user clicks the "Solve" button, the program should try to solve the remaining puzzle, i.e. place the remaining queen pieces without changing existing queen positions. (Clearly, a solution may not exist if user did not place queens correctly.)

Design:

Automation can be done if we have a clear idea about how the game is played manually. This puzzle is played in a sort of repetitive manner: every time a queen is placed, we need to find a cell where there would not be conflict.

We could use this basic understanding to design the auto mode: the program could scan the board row by row from the top; if a row is already filled (by the user) it would be skipped; the program would then place a queen in the first column (of this row) where there is no conflict. This same procedure would then repeat for the next row. If no suitable column is found, the procedure would return failure, in which case the previous row would need to adjust its choice.

This approach is called "brute force" or "exhaustive search" because we indeed try all possible moves until gold is struck. Such repetitive work is best done in a recursive manner as explained below.

See the following algorithm to understand the recursive approach better:

Solve Puzzle

This high-level function simply sets things up and makes call to the recursive procedure that actually solves the puzzle.

```
Call PlaceQueenInRow with input (row number) 1. This does all the
work.
If success, show time taken.
Else, declare "No solution could be found".
```

Place Queen In Row (recursive)

Attempt to place a queen in the given row in a non-conflicting way.

```
Input: row
Output: 0 for success, 1 for failure
If row > 8 return 0
Does this row already contain a Queen? (Presumably placed by user)
If YES,
      Recurse for row+1
      Return its return code.

For each column in this row
      Place a queen at (row, column).
      Check if it causes conflict.
      If NO,
            Recurse for row+1
            Return its return value if it's 0.
      This queen did not work, so reset the cell (remove the queen)
End for
```

```
None of the columns worked, so return 1
```

Does Row Contain Queen

Utility function to check if there is already a queen placed in the given row.

```
Input: row
Sum = 0
Add up 8 locations on "Board" starting at (row, 1)
If Sum > 0
        Return YES
Else
        Return NO
End if
```

Feature Idea # 5: Help

Provide a help screen.

Design:

This is a straightforward task. Create a "Help" sprite and display it first when Green flag is clicked. You will need to ensure all other characters/sprites hide at this time. When the user clicks to continue, hide the "help" sprite and continue the program.

Save as Program Version Final

Congratulations! You have completed all features of the game. Compare your program with my program at the link below.

File: eight-queen-final.xml

Published at Berkeley site: Eight queen

```
(https://snap.berkeley.edu/snapsource/snap.html#present:Username=abjosh
i&ProjectName=eight-queen-final)
```

How to play the game:

1. Click the "Green flag": program begins with the instruction page. Click Continue to proceed.
2. The program will draw a new, empty chessboard.
3. In the 'manual' mode, you solve the puzzle. To place or remove a queen, simply click in a cell. The placement will be allowed only if there is no conflict with the existing queens on the board.
4. If you click the "Solve" button any time, the program attempts to solve the remaining puzzle. It doesn't change the current placement of queens that you have already made. If a solution is found, the program shows how long it took to solve. If no solution can be found, it says so.
5. Click "Restart" to go to step 2 above.

Project 4: Adventures in Pen Art

Do not be afraid of perfection – you will never attain it.
– Salvador Dali

Program description

Using the Pen feature of Snap, let us attempt a few challenging designs as listed below:

1. US flag
2. Recursive painted squares design
3. Sierpinski triangles
4. Square spiral
5. Tree
6. Assorted painted designs

If you want to play with my final program to get a feel for the various designs, click the link given at the end of the chapter. Try not to peek at the scripts yet, since we want to design them ourselves below.

How to run the program:

1. Click green flag to see the names of all available designs.
2. Click one of the buttons to see the design.

Snap and CS Concepts Used

When we design this program, we will make use of the following Snap and CS concepts. Learn these concepts if you don't know them before proceeding further.

- Algorithms
    - Abstraction
    - Using algorithms
    - Designing new algorithms
- Arithmetic
    - Expressions
    - Basic operators (+, -, x, /)
- Concurrency
    - Synchronization using broadcasting
- Conditional statements:
    - Conditions: YES/NO questions
    - Relational operators (=, <, >)
    - Conditionals (IF)
    - Conditionals (If-Else)
    - Conditionals (nested)
    - Boolean operators (and, or, not)
- Divide and conquer (program design technique)
- Events
- Geometry – basic (parallel lines, square, circle, triangle, etc.)
- Geometry – advanced (TRT, spiral, super-polygons, etc.)
- Looping (iteration)
    - Looping – simple (repeat, forever)
    - Looping – nested
- Motion
    - Motion – absolute
    - Motion – relative
- Pen commands (comprehensive)
- Procedures
    - Built-in
    - User defined (custom)
    - Simple
    - With inputs

- With return value
- Program output
  - Text
- Random numbers
- Recursion
- Snap UI – special features (turbo mode, warp)
- Sequence
- Stopping scripts
- User input
  - Text
  - Click buttons
  - Input validation
- Variables
  - Simple
  - Properties (built-in)
  - Local/global scope
- XY Geometry

Square spiral:

See below:

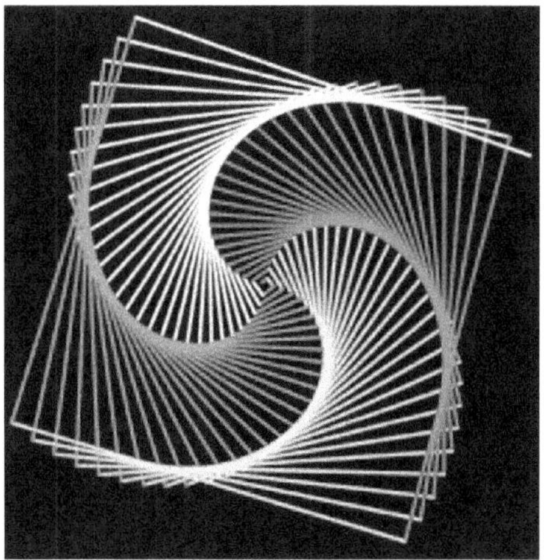

This pretty picture is actually the easiest design we will attempt in this project. It is nothing but a modification of the following design:

If you inspect it carefully, this design can be drawn using this simple algorithm:

```
Algorithm Square Spiral:
D = some small number, say 2
Repeat N times (where N is some large number like 100)
       Move D
       Turn 90
       D = D + 2
End repeat
```

To get our pretty picture, we just need to change the turning angle slightly, to, say 91. You can experiment with this further. To make it colorful, you just need to change colors alternately 4 times.

Save version final:

Congratulations! You have completed the colorful square spiral design. Compare your program with my program in the file below.

Solution: 4color-sq-spiral.xml

US Flag:

The US flag dimension specification is as follows:
(Courtesy: https://www.ushistory.org/betsy/flagetiq3.html)

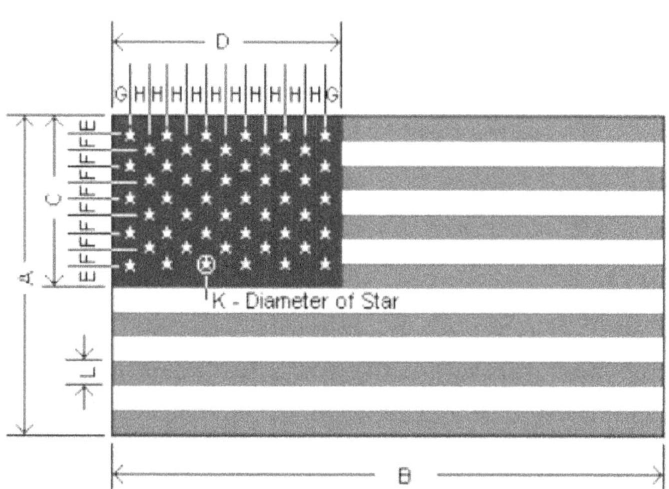

Standard proportions		
A	Hoist (width) of flag	1.0
B	Fly (length) of flag	1.9
C	Hoist (width) of Union	0.5385 (7/13)
D	Fly (length) of Union	0.76
E		0.054
F		0.054
G		0.063
H		0.063
K	Diameter of star	0.0616
L	Width of stripe	0.0769 (1/13)

We will take A as the input for the flag algorithm and calculate all other dimensions in proportion to A as specified by the table above. Let us now design our code part by part.

Star:

We need to design a filled star. There are two ways to do this. We could draw a 5-point star as shown below and fill up all the closed spaces.

```
Repeat 5
      Move 100
      Turn 144
End repeat
```

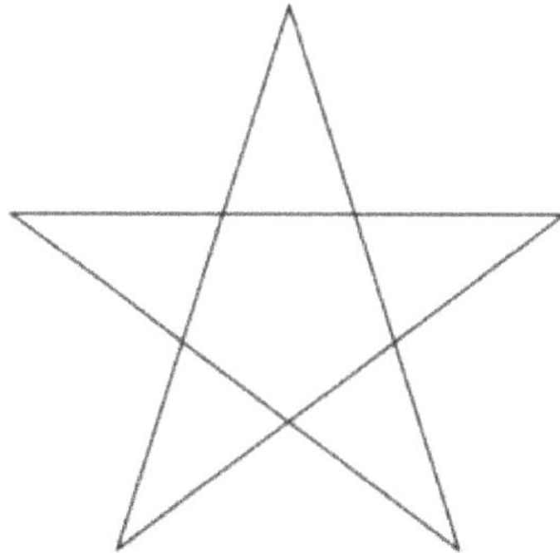

The only problem is we have to fill up 6 different spaces. An easier approach might be to draw a star as shown below so that we can fill it up easily.

How can we draw this shape? We can do it in 3 steps:
   (1) Draw a pentagon of length S
   (2) Draw a cap on top of every edge of the pentagon.
        -    Edge of the cap = (S/2) / cos72
   (3) Make the pentagon invisible (by doing "pen up")

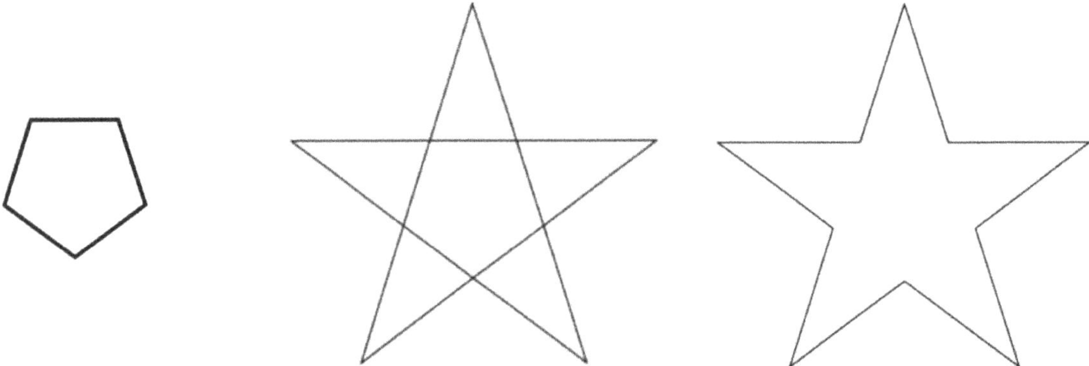

The other challenge with the filled star is that the flag specification (see above) describes its dimensions from its center, whereas we know how to draw it from one of the pentagon's vertices. See the turtle in the figure below which does the drawing for us:

So, we need to work out the geometry of moving from the center C of the star to this point A (where the turtle is).

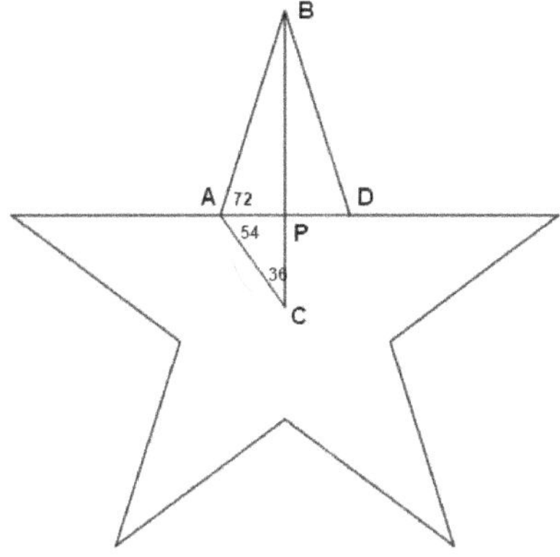

Well, our high school geometry knowledge tells us the following:
d = diameter of the star (i.e. of the circle enclosing the star) = 2 * (CP + BP)
Angle BAD = 72 (exterior angle of a pentagon)
Angle PCA = 36 (half of Angle ACD which is 360/5=72)
Angle PAC = 54
Let's denote S as the length of the pentagon (edge AD).
Then, CP = (S/2) * tan54 = 0.6882 * S
BP = (S/2) * tan72 = 1.5388 * S
Hence, d = 4.454 * S
AC = (S/2) / sin36 = 0.2939 * S

We this information, we can move the turtle from the center C to point A, draw the star and then return to the center and fill it with color.

We will put the code to draw a filled star in a custom block called FStar whose input would be the star's diameter. The caller must set the pen color before calling (in our case, i.e. for the US flag, it would be white).

Save version 1:

Congratulations! You have the "star" component figured out for the US flag. Compare your program with my program in the file below.

Solution: usflag-1.xml

Blue rectangle:

Since there are several painted rectangles in the flag, we will design a custom block called "FRectangle" which draws a painted rectangle. It will take width and height at inputs.

With this, drawing the blue rectangle is straightforward. A is the total height of the flag.

```
Frectangle(width=A*0.76, height=A*0.5385)
```

Red stripes:

There are 2 sets of red stripes. The first one consists of 4 stripes each of which can be drawn using the following call:

```
Frectangle(width=A*1.14, height=A*0.0769)
```

The gap between each pair is 0.1538.

The second set consists of 3 stripes each of which can be drawn using the following call:

```
Frectangle(width=A*1.9, height=A*0.0769)
```

Star pattern:

And now the final part is the pattern of stars. Each star can be drawn using the following call:

```
FStar( diameter = A * 0.0616 )
```

Again, there are two sets of stars:

The first set consists of 5 rows each with 6 stars. The gap between each pair of stars is A*0.126 and the gap between each pair of rows is A*0.108. We can draw this set using a nested pair of repeat loops.

The second set consists of 4 rows each with 5 stars. Except for the starting point, everything else is the same as the first set.

Here is the result of our program:

Save version final:

Congratulations! You have completed all features of the US flag. Compare your program with my program in the file below.

Solution: usflag-final.xml

Painted designs:

In this mini-project, we will attempt to draw a few interesting geometric paintings as shown below. (These are all based on concepts explained in the book "Pen Art in Snap Programming" by the same publisher.)

Let's design the shapes one by one.

Chessboard:

This is an alternating pattern of empty and filled squares. The following algorithm should take care of it:

Algorithm chessboard
```
Draw a white-painted square of the size of the entire chessboard.
Using nested looping draw a 4x4 pattern of filled squares starting row
1 and column 1 (counting from the lower-left corner). See below:
```

Draw the same 4x4 pattern starting from row 2 and column 2 (from the lower-left corner). That will give you the complete chessboard design as shown in the collage above.

The next step is to "parameterize" this design so that we can draw it at any scale. (This idea is explained in detail in the above-mentioned book.) Basically, you create a custom block with input M and use M as a multiplier for every "move" command. When M=1 it would draw as before. If M=0.5 it would draw everything at half the size and thus the entire board would half the size. And so on.

House:

We can draw this easily by breaking it down into components: wall, roof, and window. Each of them and the house itself should then be "parameterized" (using a multiplier as described above) so that we can draw the house at any scale.

Algorithm house
Draw the wall. (Square)
Draw the roof. (Sitting triangle at the top)
Draw the window. (2x2 grid of squares at the center of the wall)

Diwali lamp (also Star of David):

At first look, it may appear that there are several ways to draw this painting. For example, the easiest would be to draw two overlapped regular triangles. But, due to the peculiar way in which the FILL command works in Snap, that idea won't work. FILL only paints the smallest enclosed shape around the turtle. We need a way to draw the design in a way where every distinctly colored shape is drawn and painted separately and not through overlap.

Here is one way we can do this: Draw a hexagon star (i.e. a star superimposed on top of a hexagon) as shown below. (We have borrowed this idea from the "Pen Art" book mentioned above.)

Next, we fill the 7 separate areas with color as required.

Carrom-board design:

If you look carefully, this design only uses repetitive use of a painted square, i.e. our custom procedure `FSquare`.

Here is the basic pattern which is then repeated: (black is the background)

Algorithm Basic pattern:

```
Draw a painted square (purple)
Draw a small painted square in each corner (red)
Draw a painted square that fits among the 4 squares (turquoise)
```

Using this, we can draw the overall design as follows:

```
Draw basic pattern BA1 (colors: purple, red, and turquoise)
Draw basic pattern BA2 which fits inside BA1 (colors: turquoise, red,
and pink)
Draw basic pattern BA3 which fits inside BA2 and is rotated 90 degrees
(colors: turquoise, red, and pink)
```

Recursive Square Design:

The next few designs are based on the idea of recursion. (This idea is explained in detail in the book "Pen Art in Snap Programming" by the same publisher.)

Let us take a look at the desired end result. The following figure shows 2 possible patterns. The first one uses random colors for all squares, the second one uses some symmetry. We will first implement the first one, and then see how to achieve the color symmetry.

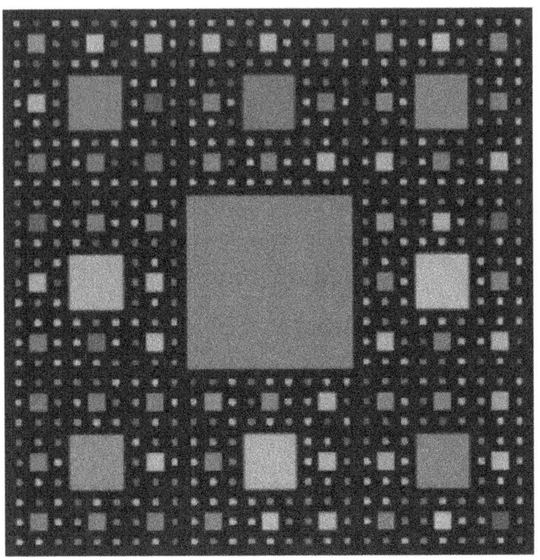 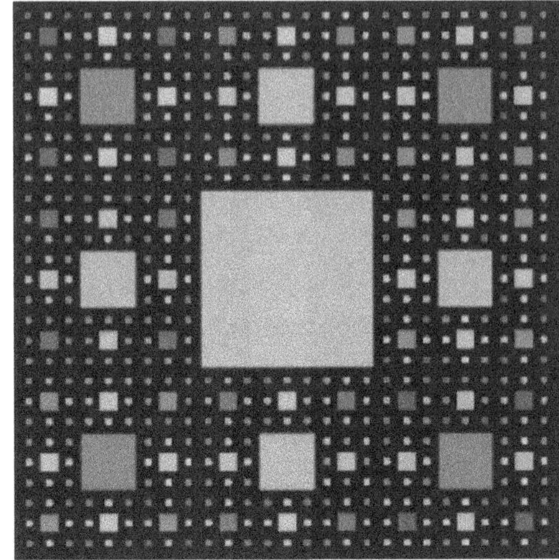

Feature Idea # 1: Basic recursive square design

Create a program that can draw the recursive squares design with random colors.

Design:

In any recursive design, the main challenge is to figure out the basic pattern. In the below design, we could imagine the basic pattern to be a big "parent" square surrounded by 8 invisible smaller "child" squares. The invisible squares get drawn in the next recursive call along with their own invisible smaller child squares. Do you get the idea?

The algorithm would be quite simple:

```
Algorithm Recursive Square Design:
Input: size S
Draw a painted square of size S with a random color.
Make 4 recursive calls with S/3 for west, north, east, and south.
(This can be a repeat loop)
Make 4 recursive calls with S/3 for northwest, northeast, southeast,
and southwest. (This can be a repeat loop)
```

Save version 1:

Congratulations! You have the basic version of the recursive square design. Compare your program with my program in the file below.

Solution: RecursiveSqDesign-1.xml

Feature Idea # 2: Symmetric recursive square design

Create a program that can draw the recursive squares design with symmetric colors.

Design:

How do we get the color symmetry as shown in the 2nd picture above?

If we allow each square to acquire its own color, it would always be random. The solution is to have the "parent" determine the color for its children and pass it as a parameter to the recursive call. See the modified algorithm below:

```
Algorithm Recursive Square Design:
Input: size S, color C
Steps:
Draw a painted square of size S with color C.
NC = random color
Make 4 recursive calls with S/3 and NC for west, north, east, and
south. (This can be a repeat loop)
NC = random color
(Note: Use different ranges for NC in Steps 2 and 4 so that all child
squares don't look identical by accident)
Make 4 recursive calls with S/3 and NC for northwest, northeast,
southeast, and southwest. (This can be a repeat loop)
```

Save version final:

Congratulations! You have the symmetric color version of the recursive square design. Compare your program with my program in the file below.

Solution: RecursiveSqDesign-final.xml

Sierpinski triangles:

This recursive design uses triangle as the basic shape. The idea of this design can be understood by examining the various depths of recursion: it is 3 regular triangles arranged as a pyramid.

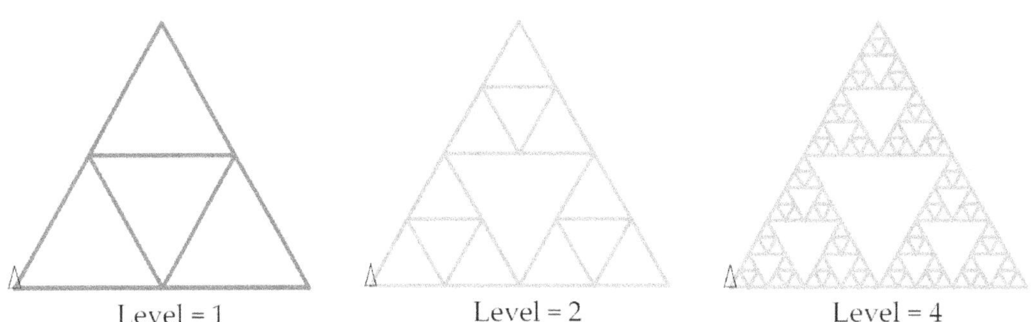

Level = 1   Level = 2   Level = 4

Feature Idea # 1: Basic Sierpinski

Create a program that can draw Sierpinski triangle with any recursive depth.

Design:

The following algorithm should do the job:

```
Algorithm Sierpinski triangle:
Input: initial size S, depth of recursion L
If L < 1
      Stop
Draw lower-left triangle with size = S/2
Recursive call with S/2 and L-1
Draw lower-right triangle with size = S/2
Recursive call with S/2 and L-1
Draw upper triangle with size = S/2
Recursive call with S/2 and L-1
Return to original position
```

Feature Idea # 2: Multi-color Sierpinski

We should be able to color the triangles with different colors.

Design:

We want to be able to create multi-color designs as shown below:

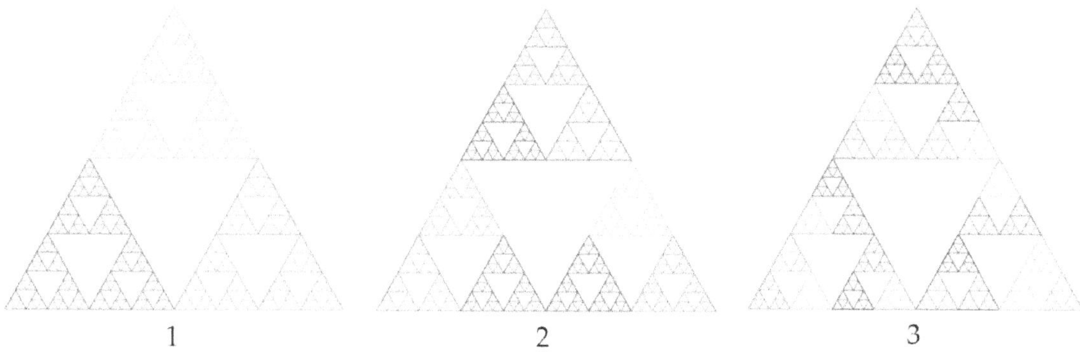

1   2   3

Let us experiment a bit to figure this out. If we set the color (randomly) at the top of the recursive procedure we will always get the 3rd pattern above, because at every level of recursion the color would be different, albeit identical for the 3 triangles at the same level.

How can we get patterns as shown in 1 or 2 above?

It almost seems as if we need a way to control at what "depth of recursion" the color should stop changing. For instance in "1" above the color change continues till recursion depth 2, in "2" the color change continues till recursion depth 3, and so on.

Does that give you an idea?

We could introduce another parameter (C) to the recursion, which can control the depth beyond which color should not change. Check out the modified algorithm below:

```
Algorithm Sierpinski multi-color triangle:
Input: initial size S, depth of recursion L, depth of color C
If L < 1
      Stop
If C > 0
      Set color randomly
Draw lower-left triangle with size = S/2
Recursive call with S/2, L-1, C-1
Draw lower-right triangle with size = S/2
Recursive call with S/2, L-1, C-1
Draw upper triangle with size = S/2
Recursive call with S/2, L-1, C-1
Return to original position
```

In this algorithm, color change would stop as soon as C reaches 0. That's how the caller can control the color variation.

Save version 1:

Congratulations! You have the basic version of a multi-color Sierpinski triangle. Compare your program with my program in the file below.

Solution: sierpinski-1.xml

Feature Idea # 3: Painted Sierpinski

Paint the triangles in the design.

Design:

We want to be able to create something like this:

As you can see, it is quite straightforward. We just need to paint the central triangle in the recursive procedure. And we pick the color at random. We will take the basic version (monochrome) and modify it:

```
Algorithm Sierpinski painted triangle:
Input: initial size S, depth of recursion L
If L < 1
     Stop
Draw the 3 triangles with size = S/2 and make recursive call for each
Move to the central triangle and fill it with a random color
```

There is a slight problem with this. We get all kinds of weird colors for the edges of the
design. See the design below closely:

This is happening because we change the pen color randomly for every fill but don't
revert back to the previous color. So the new color is used for subsequent drawing
until another fill changes it.

Here is the fixed algorithm:

```
Algorithm Sierpinski painted triangle:
Input: initial size S, depth of recursion L
If L < 1
     Stop
Draw the 3 triangles with size = S/2 and make recursive call for each
Oldcolor = current color
Move to the central triangle and fill it with a random color
Set pen color to Oldcolor
```

Save version 2:

Congratulations! You have the painted multi-color Sierpinski triangle. Compare your program with my program in the file below.

Solution: sierpinski-2.xml

Feature Idea # 3: Symmetric painted Sierpinski
Paint the triangles in the design in a symmetric manner.

Design:
We want to be able to create something like this:

In this, the colors are identical at each level of recursion. At level 1, it is red, at 2 it is green, at 3 it is turquoise, and so on. How do we achieve that?

Obviously, this is not possible if at each level the color is picked randomly. That means, a "parent level" should tell its 3 "child levels" what color they should use by passing a "color" parameter.

Here is the modified algorithm:

```
Algorithm Sierpinski symmetrically painted triangle:
Input: initial size S, depth of recursion L, color for painting C
If L < 1
      Stop
NC = pick a random color
Draw the 3 triangles with size = S/2 and
      Make recursive call for each with S/2, L-1, NC
      Revert pen color to C after each call
Move to the central triangle and paint it
```

With this algorithm, this is what we get:

As you can see, there is still a problem: the color at each level is not the same *across the entire design*. For example, at level 3 of the recursion, the color is purple in the lower-left region and green in the lower-right region. How do fix this issue?

Well, before we can fix it, we need understand why it is happening. It you look carefully, the parent level picks a color for its 3 children randomly. So, for example, at level 2, the light blue triangle at lower-left gets "purple" for its 3 children, but its peer light blue triangle at lower-right gets "green" for its 3 children! How do we ensure that "random" returns the same for both? We can't. We must think of some other means in place of random.

Here is a possible fix. Instead of using random, we will use "fixed shift" in the color value. That way, each parent will use the same shift for its children thus giving identical colors across the entire design. See the algorithm below:

```
Algorithm Sierpinski symmetrically painted triangle:
Input: initial size S, depth of recursion L, color for painting C
If L < 1
     Stop
NC = C + 23    --> 23 is arbitrary, you can use any shift value
Draw the 3 triangles with size = S/2 and
     Make recursive call for each with S/2, L-1, NC
     Revert pen color to C after each call
Move to the central triangle and paint it
```

With this magic fix, the problem is solved! The only caveat is this: you must pick the initial colors randomly if you want different colors every time you run the program. See how I would launch my program:

Save version final:

Congratulations! You have completed all above features of the Sierpinski triangle. Compare your program with my program in the file below.

Solution: sierpinski-final.xml

Beautiful trees:

One of the most interesting applications of recursion is trees – which look as natural as real trees. As you will see, designing these trees is partly programming the recursive algorithm and partly designing the appearance of the tree, and the latter is much more challenging.

The idea of designing trees using recursion has been explained in great detail in the book "Pen Art in Snap Programming" by the same publisher. We will not repeat all of the theory here, but just mention the most important details.

To write a proper recursive tree procedure, you must
- Return the Turtle to its starting position, and
- Insert recursive calls at places where you want branches to grow (usually at end-points).

For example, the following algorithm creates an asymmetric recursive tree.

```
Algorithm Recursive Tree
Input: size S, depth D
If D < 1
      Stop
Move straight up S/3
Draw a branch of length S/15 at 30 degrees on the left, and recurse
with 2S/3 and D-1
Move straight up S/6
Draw a branch of length S/15 at 25 degrees on the right, and recurse
with S/2 and D-1
Move straight up S/3
Draw a branch of length S/15 at 25 degrees on the left, and recurse
with S/2 and D-1
Move straight up S/6
Draw a branch of length S/15 at 25 degrees on the right, and recurse
with S/2 and D-1
Move straight down S
```

Note that after drawing every branch the turtle must return to the main stem (with orientation straight up), and it must return to its original position at the end.

When we run this algorithm with D=1, 3, and 6, we get the following trees.

Now you can appreciate that the key in getting a beautiful tree is in the design of the basic pattern (visible with D=1).

What we want to design is a somewhat symmetric tree with leaves and flowers. Let's go step by step.

Feature Idea # 1: A symmetric tree

Design a somewhat symmetric realistic-looking tree.

Design:

We will take the earlier algorithm above and add another parameter T for pen thickness. That way, we can show our tree with the thickness reducing as it branches deeper and deeper.

```
Algorithm Recursive Tree
Input: size S, depth D, pen thickness T
If D < 1
      Stop
Set pen size to T
Move straight up S/3
```

```
At 35 degrees on the left recurse with 2S/3, D-1, and 0.6T
Set pen size to T
At 35 degrees on the right recurse with S/3, D-1, and 0.6T
Set pen size to T
Move straight up S/4
At 25 degrees on the left recurse with S/3, D-1, and 0.6T
At 35 degrees on the right recurse with S/2 D-1, and 0.6T
Move straight up S/6
Recurse straight up with S/6, D-1, and 0.6T
Move straight down 3S/4
```

With this algorithm, we get the following patterns with D=2, 3, and 5

Save version 1:

Congratulations! You have completed the basic features of our tree. Compare your program with my program in the file below.

Solution: tree-1.xml

Feature Idea # 2: Include leaves and flowers

Make our tree have leaves and flowers.

Design:

Real trees don't have leaves all over the place, they only appear on smaller branches. To achieve the same effect, we can check the "depth of recursion" to decide whether to attach a bunch of leaves. A bunch of leaves would basically be 3 leaves connected at the base. The design of a single leaf itself we will borrow from our "Pen Art" book mentioned earlier. See below a single leaf and the "bunch of leaves" that we plan to use in our tree.

We will use a similar strategy with flowers. They usually appear only at the endpoints of branches. We can implement this by drawing flowers at the deepest level of recursion. Similar to leaves, we will draw a bunch of 3 flowers, each of which would simply be a tiny, red, filled circle.

Here is the modified algorithm for leaves and flowers.

```
Algorithm Recursive Tree
Input: size S, depth D, pen thickness T
If D < 1
      Draw a bunch of red flowers
      Stop
```

 | *Adventures in Snap Programming*

```
If D < 4
     Draw a bunch of leaves
Set pen size to T
Move straight up S/3
At 35 degrees on the left recurse with 2S/3, D-1, and 0.6T
Set pen size to T
At 35 degrees on the right recurse with S/3, D-1, and 0.6T
Set pen size to T
Move straight up S/4
At 25 degrees on the left recurse with S/3, D-1, and 0.6T
At 35 degrees on the right recurse with S/2 D-1, and 0.6T
Move straight up S/6
Recurse straight up with S/6, D-1, and 0.6T
Move straight down 3S/4
```

Save version 2:

Congratulations! You have added a few essential features to our tree. Compare your program with my program in the file below.

Solution: tree-2.xml

Feature Idea # 3: Make it more realistic

Add features to make our tree more realistic and versatile. Consider the following:

1. *Leaves should have varying shades of green.*
2. *Allow multiple colors for the leaves (including Fall colors).*
3. *Control flower density through a parameter.*
4. *Allow some variation in the overall shape of the tree every time we create it.*

Design:

Let us tackle these ideas one by one.

In Snap, "pen color" is a combination of the following factors:

- Hue
- Saturation
- Brightness
- Transparency

Each of these can vary from 1 to 100. Among these, "brightness" creates different shades of the same color. The "Leaf" custom block that draws a leaf, could pick the brightness from a range and thus draw a leaf of different shade every time.

For feature #2 above, we need to control the "hue" component of pen color. We will create a variable for this purpose, which would take some value before the program draws the tree. But, for "Fall" colors we need to make special arrangements, since these colors consist of multiple "hues". So, we will include an additional variable called "fall colors" which would be True or False. The following algorithm shows how we will handle the color and shades:

Before calling "Tree" routine:
```
If user wants Fall colors:
      Set "fall colors" to True
Else:
      Set "leaf color" to user choice
End if

...
```
In "Leaf" procedure:
```
If Fall colors = True
      Set hue = pick random (yellow to dark red)
      Set brightness = 100
Else
      Set hue = "leaf color"
      Set brightness = pick random
End if
```

How about feature #3 above? How can we control the density of flowers? Right now, we are drawing flowers at every end-point of the tree.

Imagine that there is another variable called "flower density" that takes a value from 1 to 5, 1 being for lowest density and 5 for the highest. Through this variable, we would basically like to control the likelihood of drawing a flower at an end-point.

We could consider using the "pick random" operator here. What if we modified its range using the above variable? See below:

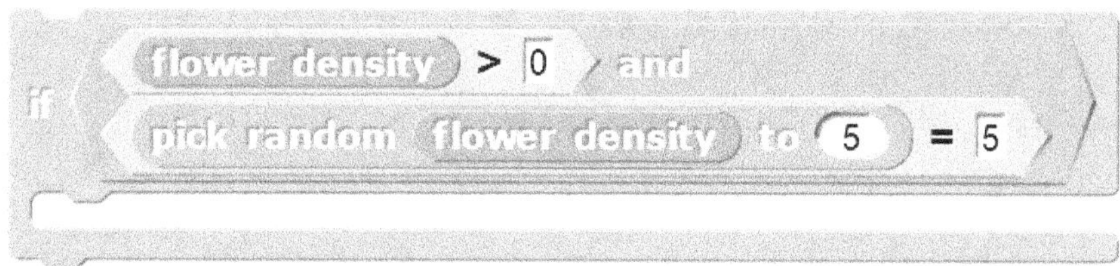

When flower density is 5, the operator would always return 5, and thus the likelihood of drawing would be 100%. When flower density is 1, the likelihood of drawing would be 20%. To include the "flowerless" appearance, we will modify this statement slightly as below.

We have thus taken care of feature #3.

Finally, for feature #4, we need to add some randomness to our tree algorithm, without completely altering its appearance ("species"). For example, we don't want it to turn into a Christmas tree by accident!

We can achieve this by introducing some "gentle randomness" at the angles where branches shoot out and for their lengths. See the modified algorithm below, for example. We will only consider the portion that draws the branches (i.e. the recursive calls).

```
Algorithm Recursive Tree
...
At (pick random 30-40) degrees on the left recurse with (pick 1/3 or
2/3)S, D-1, and 0.6T
Set pen size to T
At (pick random 33-37) degrees on the right recurse with (pick 1/3 or
2/3)S, D-1, and 0.6T
Set pen size to T
Move straight up S/4
At (pick random 23-27) degrees on the left recurse with (pick 1/3 or
2/3)S, D-1, and 0.6T
At (pick random 30-40) degrees on the right recurse with 0.5S, D-1,
and 0.6T
```

```
Move straight up S/6
Recurse straight up with (pick 1/6 or 2/6)S, D-1, and 0.6T
Move straight down 3S/4
```

You are of course free to try different values in the above randomness and get different types of variation for your tree.

Save version final:

Congratulations! You have completed the program for drawing beautiful trees! Compare your program with my program in the file below.

Solution: tree-final.xml

Save combined version:

Put all the above designs into a single program. Compare your program with my program at the file or link below.

Solution: pen-art.xml

Berkeley Snap site: Pen Art
(`https://snap.berkeley.edu/snap/snap.html#present:Username=abjoshi&ProjectName=pen-art`)

How to run the program:
1. Click green flag to see names of all available designs.
2. Click one of the buttons to see the design.

Project 5: Picture Arithmetic

Playfulness is a more important consideration than play. The former is an attitude of mind; the latter is a passing outward manifestation of this attitude.
– John Dewey

Program description

This is a simple program that allows a preschooler practice adding or subtracting single digit numbers. Basically, it presents 2 numbers in countable picture form and asks how much the sum or difference is. The user needs to perform as many operations as possible in 30 seconds. At the end the program presents the score: how many were right and wrong.

Although the program does something very simple, it requires some effort to design as described below.

Snap and CS Concepts Used

When we design this program, we will make use of the following Snap and CS concepts. Learn these concepts if you don't know them before proceeding further.

- Algorithms
- Animation using costumes
- Arithmetic
    - o   Basic operators (+, -, x, /)
- Backdrops – multiple
- Concurrency
    - o   Running scripts in parallel
    - o   Synchronization using broadcasting
- Conditional statements:
    - o   Conditions: YES/NO questions
    - o   Relational operators (=, <, >)

- o Conditionals (IF)
  - o Conditionals (If-Else)
- Data types – basic
  - o Integers
- Data types – strings
  - o String operations
- Events
- Looping (iteration)
  - o Looping - simple (repeat, forever)
  - o Looping - nested
  - o Looping - conditional (repeat until)
- Procedures
  - o Custom blocks
- Program output
  - o Text
- Random numbers
- Sequence
- STAMP - creating images
- Stopping scripts
- User input
  - o Text
- Variables
  - o Simple
  - o As timer

Explore the program:

If you want to play with my final program to get a feel for how it works, click the link given at the end of the article. Try not to peek at the scripts yet, since we want to design them ourselves below.

1. Click the "Green flag" and read the instructions.
2. Perform as many operations as you can until the timer expires.
3. The program will announce your points and stop.

High Level Design

This is where we take a step back and try to get our arms around the task of writing this program. We will first understand the basic features and the flow of operation.

Let's take a look at the main screens of the program and then work out the high level details.

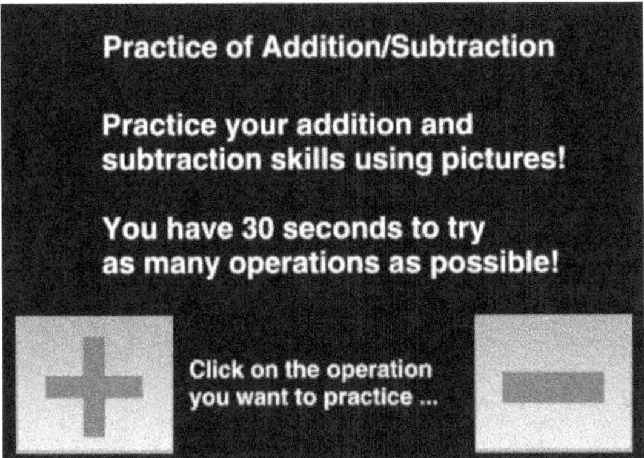

Welcome screen on which you pick what you want to practice

Actual interactive game screen

For both operations (addition and subtraction) there are two parts to our program. The back-end (or invisible) part does the following:

1. It generates 2 random numbers for each operation.
2. It verifies user's input with the actual result.
3. It repeats steps 1 and 2 until the time is up.
4. It keeps score of correct and incorrect.

The front-end does the following:

1. It presents each pair of numbers as graphical objects (animal pictures).
2. It accepts user input and passes it to the back-end.

The back-end is fairly simple: it just involves 3 variables (say X, Y, and Z) to manage each operation, and 2 more two keep the score. In addition, we will need some way to know which operation (addition or subtraction) is selected by user for practice. For this too, we can use a variable (say "operation").

For the front-end, we will use the "stamp" feature of Snap to create graphical images on the screen. Since the two numbers to be added or subtracted are single-digit, the max number of images would be 9 in the left half of the screen plus 9 in the right half. Each set of 9 images can be presented as 3 rows of 3 each. Thus, we will need a script that can manage this 3x3 grid of images.

For animal images, we could endow a single sprite with lots of animal costumes. For each operation, we could pick one of these costumes (at random) and use it to create the "stamp" images.

That is really all the work we need to do, right?

Objects:

As usual, we will use object-oriented design techniques to build our program. The first step is to list the required objects. Here is our initial list:

- Back-end logic (some invisible sprite and/or the stage)
- Animal sprite (with costumes of various animals)

Global data:

The operation type (addition or subtraction), the numbers involved for each operation and the score would all be global variables, since both front and back-end will need them.

Let us now build the program feature by feature and design the objects incrementally. We will build all backend feature ideas in the initial version and frontend ideas in the final version.

Feature idea #1: Pick the operation and initial setup

Ask user what they want to practice, and set things up.

Design:

We will include this step in the welcome/help screen of the program, as shown in one of the pictures above. The welcome screen is just a matter of creating another backdrop with the appropriate instructions. The program will present it first when Green flag is clicked.

In addition, we will have two button sprites: one for addition and one for subtraction. Here is the logic that we will use to get user's choice:

- Present welcome screen and the +/- buttons.
- Set the variable "operation" depending on which button is clicked.
- Let the backend know that selection has been made (broadcast "operation picked").
- Hide the buttons.

Subsequent game script would include the following steps:
- Initialize global variables (score, timer, etc.)
- Let everyone know game is about to start (broadcast).
- Run the game loop until timer expires.

Feature idea #2: The backend logic
Create code for the backend object to create numbers for each round and keep score. Ask user for each round. Present the final score.

Design:
We will use the stage to host the backend logic.

Let's consider each operation separately.

Logic for "addition" practice:
- Create 2 random numbers X, Y (in the range 1 to 9) for each round and calculate their sum Z.
- Ask frontend to display the numbers and get user input.
- Compare Z with user's input. Keep score and present it after timer loop is finished.

Logic for "subtraction" practice:

- For each round: (a) Create random number X in the range 1 to 9. (b) Create random number Y in the range 1 to X because we always want X-Y to be 0 or positive. (c) Calculate Z = X - Y.
- Ask frontend to display the numbers and get user input.
- Compare Z with user's input. Keep score and present it after timer loop is finished.

Save as Program Version 1

Let's save this project before continuing to the remaining ideas. Compare your program with my program below.

Solution: picture-arithmetic-1.xml

How to run the program:
1. Click on the "Green flag" and read the instructions.
2. Perform as many additions/subtractions as you can until the timer expires.
3. The program will announce your points and stop.

Final Version

In this next version of the program, we will work on the following feature ideas:
- Create code for the front-end, i.e. code to create animal images to represent the numbers to be added or subtracted.

Feature idea #3: Graphic animal images

Create animal images to represent the two numbers to be added or subtracted.

Design:
There are two parts to this presentation.

Part 1: Present the appropriate symbol + or – depending on the selected operation.

This part is easy. As soon as the game begins, everyone will get a "start game" message. By looking at the global variable "operation" the appropriate button sprite (used in Feature #1 above) will show itself at the center of the screen.

We also need to make another small change. These buttons will need to ignore the "click" event (in case anyone clicks by mistake) because it has no role during practice. This can be achieved by checking the current position or size of the sprite since presumably both of these properties would be different from the "welcome" screen. See the modified script below:

```
If button clicked:
If size as expected for "welcome" screen
     <previous steps>
End if
```

Part 2: Present the numbers X and Y using images.

As mentioned earlier, we will use a single sprite and use its costumes to create the graphic images. We will use the "stamp" feature of Snap to create multiple images on the screen. Each number would be presented as a 3x3 grid of images, since it would be between 1 and 9.

Since there are 2 numbers, we would use the same code to draw the first number in the left half of the screen and the second number in the right half.

The main challenge is to work out the algorithm for setting up animal images in a 3x3 grid pattern. For example, if the number is 4, we need to draw one row of 3 images followed by another row of 1 image. If the number is 7, we need to draw two rows of 3 images each followed by a row of 1 image.

Here is one possible algorithm:

```
Input: N (number 1 to 9)

Y = starting Y position of top row
Repeat until N = 0
     X = starting X position of a row
     If N <= 3
           Paint a row of N images using STAMP
           N = 0
     Else
           Paint a row of 3 images using STAMP
```

```
          N = N - 3
      End if
      Y = Y - row size
End repeat
```

Feature idea #4: Custom block

Convert the script for drawing images into a custom Snap procedure.

Design:

Use N (the number to be shown) and location (starting X value of the 3x3 grid) as inputs to this procedure. Use script (local) variables for all temporary calculations and data.

Save as Program Version "Final"

Congratulations! You have completed all the main features of the program. Compare your program with my program in the file below.

Solution: picture-arithmetic-final.xml

Also available at the Berkeley Snap website: Picture arithmetic
`(https://snap.berkeley.edu/snap/snap.html#present:Username=abjoshi&ProjectName`
`=picture-arithmetic-final)`

How to run the program:
1. Click on the "Green flag" and follow the instructions.
2. Perform as many additions/subtractions as you can until the timer expires.
3. The program will announce your points and stop.

Project 6: Bubble Sort

Programming is the activity by which people can convey their abstract ideas to computers. In that sense, computer programs are simulation of ideas – simple or complex.
– Abhay B. Joshi

Program description

Sorting numbers is a classical problem in Computer Science which involves arranging a set of numbers in increasing or decreasing order. There are several popular algorithms to do this, and "Bubble Sort" is one such technique. In this program, we will simply use the bubble sort algorithm and create a graphical simulation to show how it works.

We will use an array of numbers (say 1 to 20). Associated with each number there will be a vertical bar. The pipe's length will be proportional to the number.

The program will let you shuffle the array and then sort it using the bubble sort algorithm. The bars will visually depict how the numbers move around in the array.

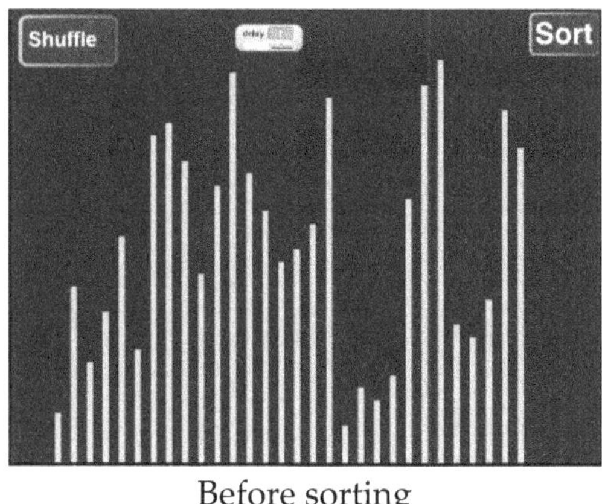

Before sorting

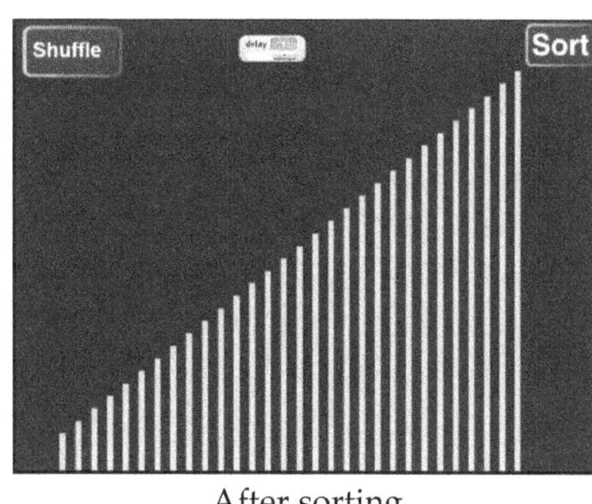

After sorting

The above pictures show the simulation of sorting, where the first picture shows the numbers out of order and the second picture shows them in an increasing order.

Snap and CS Concepts Used

When we design this program, we will make use of the following Snap and CS concepts. Learn these concepts if you don't know them before proceeding further.

- Algorithms
    - o Using algorithms
- Animation using costumes
- Arithmetic
    - o Expressions
    - o Basic operators (+, -, x, /)
    - o Advanced operators: mod, floor, ceiling, etc.
- Concurrency
    - o Synchronization using broadcasting
- Conditional statements:
    - o Conditions: YES/NO questions
    - o Relational operators (=, <, >)
    - o Conditionals (IF)
    - o Conditionals (If-Else)
    - o Conditionals (nested IF)
    - o Boolean operators (and, or, not)
- Data structures – list
    - o List operations
- Data types – basic
    - o Integers
- Data types – strings
    - o String operations (join, letter, length of)
- Looping (iteration)
    - o Looping - simple (repeat, forever)
    - o Looping - conditional (repeat until)
- OOP
    - o Clones
- Procedures

- Built-in
    - User defined (custom)
    - Simple
    - With inputs
- Random numbers
- Sequence
- User input
    - Text
    - Click buttons
- Variables
    - Simple
    - Properties (built-in)
    - Local/global scope

Explore the program:

If you want to play with my final program to get a feel for how it works, click the link given at the end of the article. Try not to peek at the scripts yet, since we want to design them ourselves below.

1. Click the "Green flag": A sorted (in ascending order) array of numbers will be created. The pipes displayed on the screen will be sorted accordingly.
2. Click the "Shuffle" button: the list will be shuffled. The pipes displayed on the screen will be shuffled accordingly.
3. Click the "Sort" button: Start sorting the list. For each comparison the pipes will be colored, for each swap the pipes will be swapped.

High Level Design

This is where we take a step back and try to get our arms around the task of writing this program. We will first understand the basic features and the flow of operation.

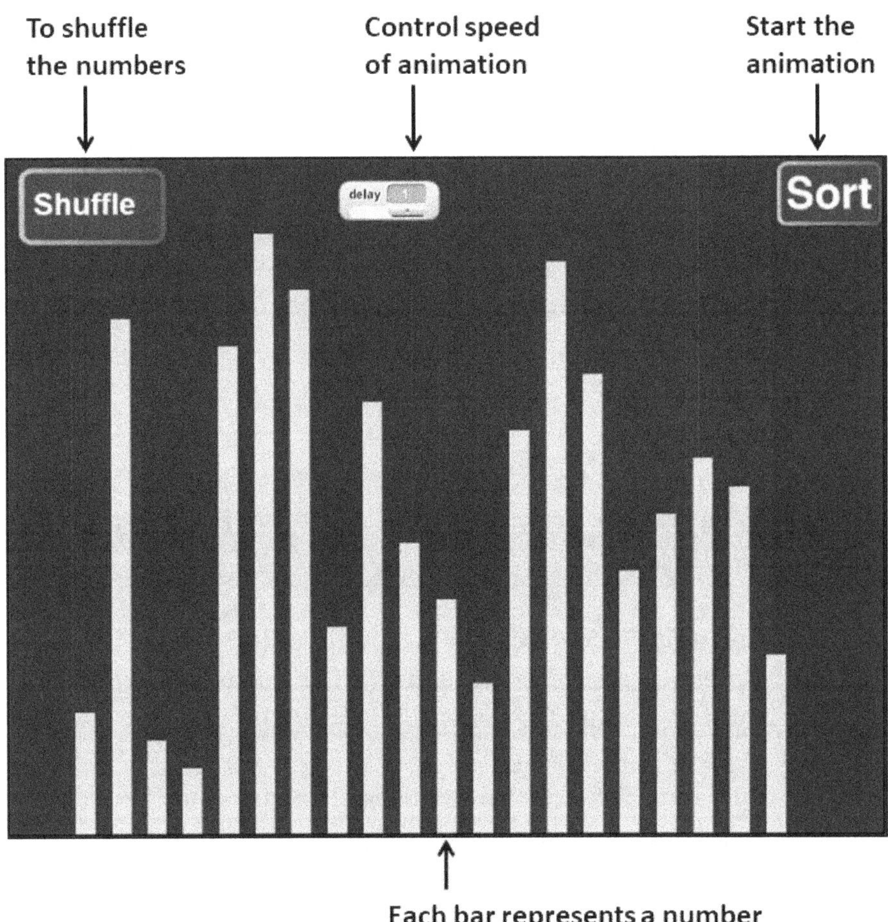

There are two parts to our program. The back-end (or invisible) part does the actual shuffling and sorting of numbers. The front-end consists of vertical bars that represent the numbers as they are shuffled and sorted.

For the backend, we will use the standard Bubble Sort algorithm given at https://en.wikipedia.org/wiki/Bubble_sort.

Since we are sorting numbers, we will use a list to hold these numbers.

For the front-end, we will use vertical bars to represent the numbers. Since all bars are identical except their height, we will use a single "bar sprite" and clone it as needed. But, how will we vary the height of each clone? We will use a visual trick: each bar would actually have the same height (the same as Snap vertical height), but the bar could be *vertically positioned* such that it *appears* short or tall.

We could design the back-end first, that is, create all the logic of the number list, shuffling the numbers, and running the sorting algorithm on the list, etc. We could then design the front-end, that is, create the bar sprite, create its clones (as many as the numbers in the list), and position them on the screen such that they correctly represent the numbers. Finally, we could put in code which synchronizes movement of bars concurrently with the shuffling and sorting of numbers.

Objects:

As usual, we will use object-oriented design techniques to build our program. The first step is to list the required objects. Here is our initial list:

- Back-end logic (some invisible sprite)
- Bar
- Click-buttons to "shuffle" and "sort"

Global data:

We will have a List called "L" to hold the array of numbers.

Let's now build the program feature by feature and design the objects incrementally.

Initial Version

In the initial version of the program, we will work on the following feature ideas:
- Add code to the back-end object to shuffle and sort a list of numbers.
- Add "shuffle" and "sort" click-buttons for user to request these operations.

Feature idea #1: The back-end logic
Create logic to build the list of numbers, shuffle it, and sort it using Bubble Sort.

Design:

***Step 1**: Create custom blocks as per the algorithms below.*

Shuffle list:
(adapted Donald Knuth's algorithm)
```
I = 0
Repeat N times:
      Pick a random integer R such that 0 <= R <= N-I-1
      T = I + R
      Swap numbers between locations T+1 and I+1
End repeat
```

Bubble sort:
(N is size of number array. Assuming number array base is 1)
```
i = N + 1
Repeat until i=1
      Newi = 1
      j = 2
      Repeat until j = i
            If A[j-1] > A[j] then
                  Swap( A[j-1], A[j] )
                  Newi = j
            End if
            j = j + 1
      End repeat
      i = Newi
End repeat
```

***Step 2**: Create logic to build a list of numbers and sort it.*

The list L will initially be loaded with numbers from 1 to N where N is specified by the user (via the ASK command). Obviously the list will be sorted initially. When user clicks the Shuffle button the "shuffle" algorithm above will ruin this order. When user clicks the Sort button we will pass L through the "bubble sort" algorithm to sort it again.

Snap allows you to make the list visible so that the user can see all the operations in action.

Feature idea #2: Shuffle and Sort buttons
Create buttons using which user can shuffle or sort the list.

Design:
We will use two new objects: shuffle and sort button sprites whose job simply is to send messages when they are clicked.

Save as Program Version 1
Let's save this project before continuing to the remaining ideas. Compare your program with my program below.

Solution: BubbleSort-1.xml

How to run the program:
1. Click on the "Green flag" to initialize the list of numbers.
2. Click "Shuffle" to shuffle the list.
3. Click "Sort" to sort the list.

Final Version
In this next version of the program, we will work on the following feature ideas:
- Create vertical bars that represent each number in the list.
- Make the bars move on the screen when the numbers are moved within the list (during shuffling or sorting).
- Provide a way to control the speed of movement of bars.
- Highlight the bars being swapped so that the user can see how the bubble sort algorithm works.

Feature idea #3: Vertical bars

Create vertical bars that represent each number in the list.

Design:

As mentioned earlier, we will use a single bar sprite and use its clones to represent the numbers. This is a vertical bar as high as the screen. It should hide somewhere so that it doesn't interfere with its clones. All its clones will be positioned on X axis. Each bar will have unique X and Y positions. Once created, the Y position of each bar remains unchanged throughout the program.

Let us try to understand what each clone needs to know and do.

Step 1: During setup arrange the bars left to right on the screen.

Arrange such that the first bar will represent the first number in the list, the second bar will represent the second number in the list, and so on. We will spread out the bars to cover most of the screen.

Design:

We can achieve this by having each clone calculate its "x position", which should be straightforward. We know the total screen width available and also the width of each bar, using which we can calculate the x position of each bar such that they are all evenly placed from left to right.

We can also have each clone calculate its height (i.e. its "y position") by looking at the number it represents. This should also be straightforward. Basically the y position will increase evenly from 1 to N.

Step 2: Relate each clone with its associated number in the list L.

That is, how would a clone know which number it represents?

Design:

We have two options: one is to save the number itself as a "private variable" of the clone, or, save the location (aka index) of the number in list L. If you think about these options carefully, it is clear that the latter option is better, because using the index we can quickly find the number, but the other way round is not so easy.

Step 3: *During shuffling and sorting, move the bars as their corresponding numbers move in the list.*

Design:

After a careful study of the shuffling and sorting algorithms, it is clear that the movement of bars happens when a pair of numbers is "swapped". That means a pair of corresponding bars would be swapped on the screen.

Every time a swap happens in the list, we could save the two indexes in a couple of global variables swap1 and swap2 and send a broadcast. Every clone will then check if its own index matches one of these two. If it does, it will save the other index as its own and recalculate its new "x position".

Go ahead and write the above scripts for the "bar" object.

Feature idea #4: Delay and highlight

Since the main purpose of this program is to learn about the Bubble Sort algorithm, it would be nice to able to watch the algorithm in slow motion.

Step 1: *Add the feature to control the speed of every swap.*

Design:

This can be achieved by having a slider variable called "delay" and using "glide" instead of "go to x y" when we move the bars.

The problem is this will also slow down the "shuffling" of bars, which we are not really interested in watching in slow motion. The easy fix for this is to set the delay to 0 temporarily during shuffling.

Step 2: *Highlight the pair of bars which has been selected to be swapped.*

Design:

This can be achieved by having the selected bars change their color before the swap and resetting it after.

<u>Step 3</u>: *Vary the thickness of bars based on the total count. The bars should be thinner if the count is large and thicker if the count is small.*

Design:

Since there is no way in Snap to resize only the thickness of bars, we will use 3 separate costumes to accommodate different ranges. One is for 5 to 20, second is 20 to 50, and third is 50 to 100. The choice of the appropriate costume would be made during setup.

Save as Program Version "Final"

Congratulations! You have completed all the main features of the program. Compare your program with my program at the link below.

Solution: BubbleSort-final.xml

Also available at the Berkeley Snap website: Bubble sort
(`https://snap.berkeley.edu/snapsource/snap.html#present:Username=abjoshi&Proje ctName=BubbleSort-final`)

How to run the program:

1. Click the "Green flag": A sorted (in ascending order) array of numbers will be created. The bars displayed on the screen will be sorted accordingly. Set the "delay" slider appropriately.
2. Click the "Shuffle" button: the list will be shuffled. The bars displayed on the screen will be shuffled accordingly.
3. Click the "Sort" button: Start sorting the list. For each comparison the bars will be colored, for each swap the bars will be swapped.

Project 7: Sliding Numbers

Mathematics provides a framework for dealing precisely with notions of "what is".
Computation provides a framework for dealing precisely with notions of "how to".
— Hal Abelson

Program description

This is a game you play with a grid with numbered blocks. One of the cells is empty, so that neighboring blocks can slide to it. The goal of the game is to line up the numbers left-to-right and top-to-bottom. The following picture shows a 4x4 grid with numbers 1 thru 15.

We will write a program that implements a 3x3 grid containing numbers 1 thru 8. So the game would involve starting with a jumbled set of numbers 1 thru 8 and then ordering them.

Explore the game:

If you want to play with my final program to get a feel for this game, click the link given at the end of the chapter. Try not to peek at the scripts yet, since we want to design them ourselves below.

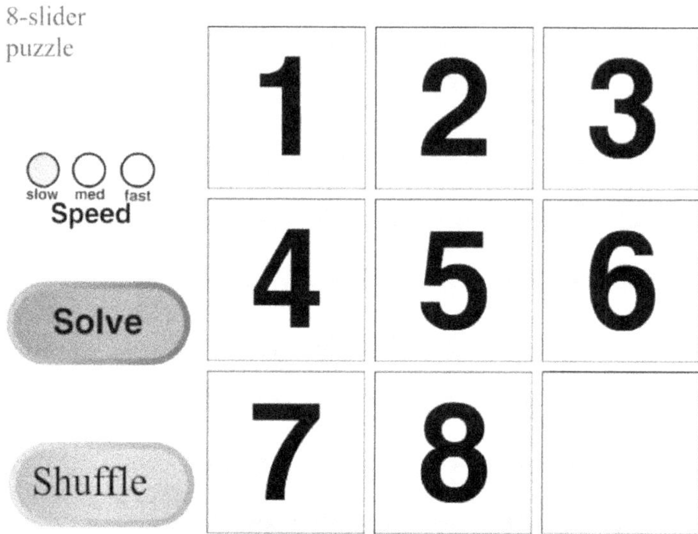

How to play the game:

1. Click the "Green flag": everything is reset to the original state.
2. Click "Shuffle" to get a shuffled state, i.e. the numbers won't be in order.
3. Click any neighboring cell (of the blank square) to swap its position with the blank square. Solve the puzzle by arranging numbers 1 thru 8 in order.
4. Or, ask the program any time to solve the puzzle by clicking "solve".

Snap and CS Concepts Used

When we design this program, we will make use of the following Snap and CS concepts. Learn these concepts if you don't know them before proceeding further.

- Algorithms
  - Abstraction
  - Designing new algorithms

- o Pseudo-code
- Animation using costumes
- Arithmetic
  - o Expressions
  - o Basic operators (+, -, x, /)
- Concurrency
  - o Synchronization using broadcasting
- Conditional statements:
  - o Conditions: YES/NO questions
  - o Relational operators (<, >, =)
  - o Conditionals (IF)
  - o Conditionals (If-Else)
  - o Conditionals (nested IF)
  - o Boolean operators (and, or, not)
- Data structures – list
  - o List operations
  - o Using list as 2-D array
  - o List traversal
- Data types – basic
  - o Integers
- Data types – strings
  - o String operations (join)
- Divide and conquer (program design technique)
- Events
- Looping (iteration)
  - o Looping - simple (repeat, for)
  - o Looping - nested
  - o Looping - conditional (repeat until)
- Motion
  - o Motion - absolute
- OOP
  - o Clones
  - o Clones differentiation: using private id
- Procedures
  - o Built-in
  - o User defined (custom)

- o Simple
  - o With inputs
  - o With return value
- Program output
  - o Text
- Random numbers
- Sequence
- User input
  - o Click buttons
- User interface elements
  - o Button
  - o Grid
- Variables
  - o Simple
  - o Properties (built-in)
  - o Local/global scope
- XY Geometry

High Level Design

This is how the main screen of my program looks like.

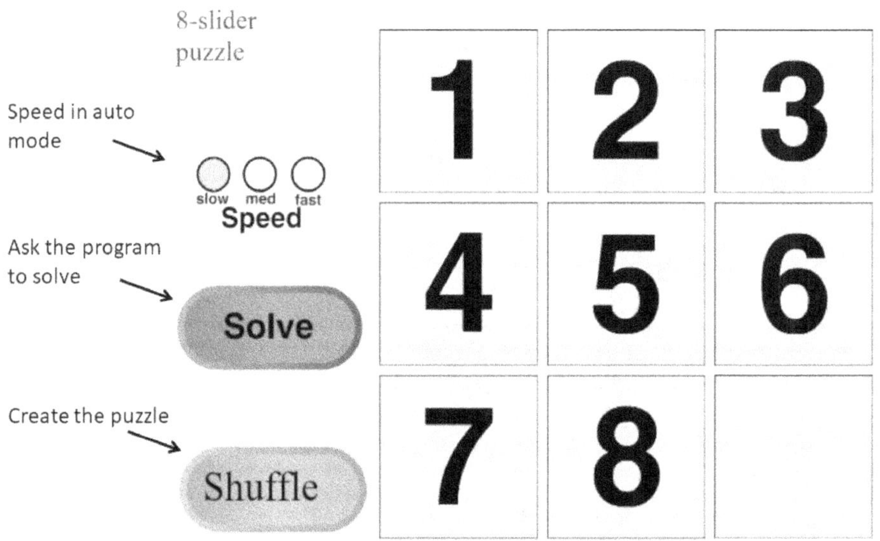

If you take a step back and think about how we can implement this program, the following ideas come to mind:

- We will need a way to track the 3x3 grid of numbers: both visually and in the backend.
- Each move will involve swapping of two cells: again both visually and in the backend.
- Shuffling can be thought be as a series of random swaps.
- For the "auto" mode we could keep a record of all moves made by "shuffle" and then replay those moves in the reverse order.

Let us now consider how we can manage the various types of data required in this program.

Data structures:

We will use a 2-D list called "grid" to save the arrangement of the numbers in the puzzle. We will use "9" to denote the empty cell. Initially, the grid would contain numbers 1 thru 9 (1,2,3,4,5,6,7,8,9) since that is how the grid is displayed at the start. Every time there is a change, i.e. when cells move around, the grid will change accordingly. For example, if "6" moves in the place of the blank cell, the grid will have 1,2,3,4,5,9,7,8,6.

Each cell (clone) will need to know its position in this grid. For this purpose, each clone will have private variables called "row" and "column".

Global variables:

The above-mentioned lists would need to be global since the whole program will need to access them.

In addition, we will need global variables to give information about (location etc.) the blank cell and information about the most recent clicked cell. Why do we need these global variables? Well, because each cell movement is going to be a swap of cells, and so, we will need this information to implement the swap both physically (on the screen) and in the grid.

Initial Version

In the initial version of the program, we will work on the following feature ideas:

- Draw a 3x3 table:
    o Each cell should be numbered 1 thru 8 with the last one being blank.
    o Make each cell interactive, i.e. it should respond to the click event.
    o Keep track of the arrangement of numbers.
- When a cell is clicked it should swap places with the blank square.

Feature Idea # 1: Square grid

Set up a 3x3 square grid showing 9 blank cells.

Design:

We will start with an earlier program called **Matrix** (from the book "Practice CS Concepts with Snap", it's called *matrix-2*). This program allows drawing a square grid (of blank squares) of any dimension. It uses clones to represent each cell. We will adapt (simplify) this program for a 3x3 table and remove all unnecessary code and variables.

(Note: The *Matrix* program is available in the files provided with this book.)

Feature Idea # 2: Numbered square grid

Load the above 3x3 square grid with numbers 1 thru 8.

Design:

Since we are using clones of a single sprite to show all 9 squares, we will use costumes to show numbers 1 thru 8 (plus one for the blank square). Costumes 1 thru 8 will actually show numbers 1 thru 8. Costume 9 will show a blank square. To ensure each clone remembers its id (i.e. the value 1 thru 9, 9 being for the blank), we will use a private variable called "cellid". During clone creation, the id will be saved in this own variable.

Feature Idea # 3: Swap cells on click

When a cell is clicked it should swap places with the blank square.

Design:

Swapping the clicked cell with the blank cell will basically require us to know the (x, y) location of the two cells. We could ask the blank cell to save its (x, y) in a pair of global variables, blankX and blankY, and the clicked cell would know its own (x, y) through the Snap properties "x position" and "y position".

In addition, the two cells must update the "grid" data structure with their new positions.

For swapping two cells we can use the following algorithm:

```
When clicked:
Record x, y coordinates of clicked cell (in a pair of global
variables)
Record row, column of clicked cell (in a pair of global variables)
Clicked cell will move to blank cell's (x, y)
Copy row, column of blank cell in private variables
Ask blank cell to move which will result in the following actions by
the blank cell:
        Blank cell will move to clicked cell's (x, y)
        Copy row, column of clicked cell in private variables
        Update global variables with the new information
Update "grid" with the new positions of the clicked and blank cell
```

Note:

Broadcast will be received by all clones. Clones decide whether to process a message by looking at their cell ids.

Save program version 1:

Congratulations! You have completed all the features listed so far. As before, let's save this project before continuing to further ideas. Compare your program with my program in the file below.

File: 8-slider-1.xml

How to play the game:

1. Click on the "Green flag": everything is reset to the original state.
2. Click any cell to swap its position with the blank square.

Next Set of Features/ideas:
- When clicked check if clicked cell is valid (i.e. suitable for the purpose of sliding).
- Provide the feature to shuffle the cells to start a new game.

Feature Idea # 4: Check if neighbor of blank cell

In the real game, the player is allowed to click only on the immediate neighbors (except those placed diagonally) of the blank square. Figure out a way to check if the given cell is a neighbor or not.

Design:

We will need to identify the 4 (max) neighbors of the blank square. The cells crossed below are the neighbors:

We can determine whether or not a cell is a neighbor of the blank cell by comparing its distance from the blank cell in "grid". Here is the algorithm to check if the given cell is a neighbor of the blank cell:

Algorithm Is Blank Neighbor:
```
Given:
Row, column of clicked cell: row1, col1: input parameters
Row, column of clicked cell: row2, col2: global variables

If row1 = row2 AND absolute(col1 - col2) = 1
      Return True
Else if col1 = col2 AND absolute(row1 - row2) = 1
```

```
      Return True
Else
      Return False
End if
```

Implement this function and call it from the script "when cell clicked".

Feature Idea # 5: Placement of cells
The real puzzle requires us to have a shuffled state. Shuffle the cells.

Design:
The actual puzzle requires a shuffled initial state. There are two ways to do this. One is
to do random placement of the numbers when we build the 3x3 grid. But it has been
shown (source: Wikipedia) that not all initial number arrangements of this puzzle are
solvable. So, we will use the second approach, in which we will initially present the
solved puzzle in which numbers 1 thru 8 appear in order followed by the blank cell.
We will then shuffle the numbers by picking cells randomly and actually sliding them.
This way, it is guaranteed that the shuffled arrangement does have a solution.

When we randomly pick cells, it would be best to pick one of the "neighbor" cells of
the blank cell because only neighbor cells can be moved. So, as a first step we will need
to continuously keep track of the neighbors of the blank cell. We will use the list
variable "neighbors" for this purpose.

Data structures:
We will use a list called "neighbors" that will have a list of the current neighbors of the
blank cell. If the blank cell moves, this list must be refreshed.

<u>Step 1</u>: *Find neighbors of the blank cell and save them in a list.*

Design:
One challenge with clones is that every broadcast message is received by every clone.
So if a message is not intended for all clones, we must have a way to restrict its
processing. This is easily accomplished thru the "cell id" which is unique for each
clone.

The task of listing neighbors of the blank cell is best given to the parent of all clones.

The parent's id is 0. The parent will simply send the message "Are you a neighbor" to all clones. Each clone will then use the function "Is Blank Neighbor" which we designed earlier. See below

```
Algorithm Are you a neighbor (all clones):
Given: list "neighbors"
If "Is blank neighbor" returns True
      Add cell id to list "neighbors"
End if
```

After all clones have responded, we will have a list of the neighbors of the blank cell. This procedure should be called every time the blank cell moves.

Step 2: *Create a new custom block for the above script (cell swap).*

Design:

The actions taken for swapping a clicked cell are identical to what we need to do a "simulated click", that is the move initiated by our shuffling procedure. To avoid duplication of code, we will create a new procedure (Snap block) called "Swap Cell".

Instead of creating a new block we could have also used a broadcast script for this common code. Converting the script into a procedure (new block) has this advantage: the broadcast script, since it runs on an event (broadcast message) would be run by all clones, whereas the new procedure would only be run by the calling clone.

Step 3: *Shuffle the cells.*

Design:

Algorithm to shuffle:
We will simulate clicks on randomly picked neighbor cells for a large number of times.

```
Repeat 100
      pseudoClick = pick at random one of the neighbor cells
      Ask this cell to move by sending the "Simulated click" message
End-repeat
```

Save program version 2:

Congratulations! You have completed all the features listed so far. As before, let's save this project before continuing to the advanced ideas. Compare your program with my program in the file below.

File: 8-slider-2.xml

How to play the game:
1. Click the "Green flag": everything is reset to the original state.
2. Click "Shuffle" to get a shuffled state, i.e. the numbers won't be in order.
3. Click any neighboring cell (of the blank square) to swap its position with the blank square. Solve the puzzle by arranging number 1 thru 8 in order.

Final Set of Features/ideas:

Include the advanced feature of "auto" mode in which the program can solve the puzzle. Design details are discussed in the feature below.

Feature Idea # 7: The "auto" mode

Can your program solve the puzzle?

Step 1: Include a "Solve" button clicking which will make the program to solve the puzzle.

Design:

So far, we expect the user to do all the clicking to try to solve the puzzle. It would be nice to include a "solve" button that will make the program solve the puzzle.

This sounds daunting but is really quite straightforward. Remember that we start the puzzle in a "solved" state and then through "shuffle" we ruin its order. If we save all the moves made by "shuffle" we just need to unroll those steps in the reverse order and we will get the solution! To this main idea we will need to include a few minor tweaks to make it robust as discussed below.

Data structures:

We will need a list called "solution" to list the numbers that need to be clicked to reach the solution of the puzzle.

See below the algorithmic outline of the auto feature:

The "auto" mode:
```
1.  Save all moves during "shuffle". Save in list "solution".
2.  When user clicks "solve":
     -   Unwind this "solution" list bottom-up. Simulate a click for each
         move just like we do in "shuffle".
     -   Empty "solution" list.
3.  What if user plays manually:
     -   Add these moves to "solution".
```

There is a small optimization we can make to this idea. If you inspect the "solution" list created by "shuffle" sometimes the list has meaningless moves (because it uses random operator which is not intelligent at all). See the example below which shows a subset of this list.

```
5
6
6
5
7
8
8
```

Each item in the list indicates which cell was moved. Now, moves 2 and 3 are meaningless because a single piece was moved back and forth. Same problem with moves 6 and 7.

Such "null" moves should ideally be deleted from the list, right? In fact, this "optimization" may need to be done repeatedly, because, as in the example above, after the 1st pass the list would have 5 repeated at 1 and 2.

Here is the algorithm for the optimization.

Algorithm Optimize
```
Call RemoveNullMoves (below) repeatedly until it returns False
```

```
Algorithm Remove Null Moves
Purpose: If an item is repeated in "L", remove both instances
Input: list L
Output: True if duplicates were found, False otherwise
Found = False
I = 1
Size = length of L
Repeat until I >= Size
        Item1 = item at I
        Item2 = item at I+1
        If Item1 = Item2
                Delete Item1 and Item2 from L
                Size = Size - 2
                I = I - 1
                Found = True
        End if
        I = I + 1
End repeat
Return Found
```

Step 2: _Include a radio control to select the speed of cell moves in the auto mode._

Design:

Users may want to see the auto mode in slow-motion so they understand the moves, or they may want to just zip through it. We will take the "radio button" control from our library (by importing _radio.xml_) and use it as is. This is what the radio sprite looks like:

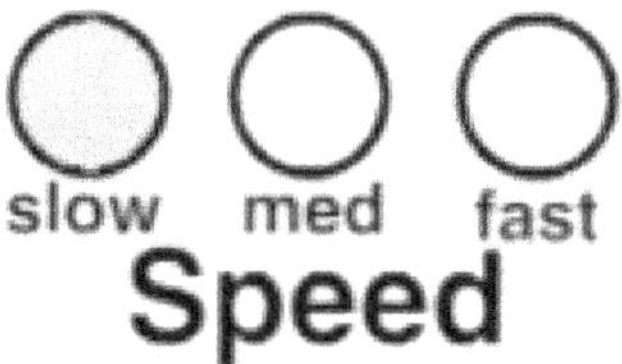

It allows you to select one of 3 speeds: slow, medium, fast

Each click sends out an appropriate message. For example, if you click on "slow" the sprite sends "speed slow" message.

How to use the control:
1. Import the sprite into your program by importing *radio.xml*.
2. Place the sprite at a suitable place with NO change in its orientation or size.
3. Have the "Solve" button sprite process the 3 messages "speed slow", "speed medium", and "speed fast" to adjust the wait time between swaps.

Save as Program Version "Final"

Congratulations! You have completed all the main features of the game. Compare your program with my program below.

Solution: 8-slider-final.xml
Link on Berkeley website: Slider puzzle final
(`https://snap.berkeley.edu/snapsource/snap.html#present:Username=abjoshi&ProjectName=8-slider-final`)

How to play the game:
1. Click the "Green flag": everything is reset to the original state.
2. Click "Shuffle" to get a shuffled state, i.e. the numbers won't be in order.
3. Click any neighboring cell (of the blank square) to swap its position with the blank square. Solve the puzzle by arranging number 1 thru 8 in order.
4. Or, ask the program to solve the puzzle any time by clicking "solve".

Further challenge

See if you can extend this program for a 4x4 grid with numbers 1 thru 15 (as shown in the picture at the very top of this document).

Project 8: Escape from the Zoo

The beautiful thing about learning is that no one can take it away from you.
– B. B. King

Program description

This program is once again based on a real board game in which there is a sort of "zoo" in which animals are trapped. The aim of the game is to free all animals from the zoo (which looks like a grid). Animals can escape, one at a time, from the gate at the far right of each row. As usual, they must follow certain rules as listed below:

Rules:

1. An animal can exit the zoo only if there is no one in front of it in its own row.
2. An animal can exit the zoo only if its color or species matches with the last animal in the free queue below the zoo.

Here is how the zoo might look like (the layout of animals would be different every game).

In our program, you can click to free these animals from the zoo one at a time. Each clicked animal lines up in a "freedom queue" below the grid.

Our 4x4 zoo contains 16 animals:
4 animal types (species): crab, dinosaur, dog, penguin
4 animal colors: red, blue, yellow, green

These animals are randomly placed all facing east.

The picture below shows a snapshot of the game after having played partially.

If you want to play with my final program to get a feel for this game, click the link given at the end of the article. Try not to peek at the scripts yet, since we want to design them ourselves below.

How to run the program:
1. Click green flag or "New Game" to start playing. Press 'h' to see help.
2. Play the game yourself by clicking on the animals. Your aim is to free all animals from the zoo (the grid).
3. Press "s" any time to let the computer try to solve the puzzle.

Snap and CS Concepts Used

When we design this program, we will make use of the following Snap and CS concepts. Learn these concepts if you don't know them before proceeding further.

- Algorithms
    - o Abstraction
    - o Using algorithms
    - o Designing new algorithms
    - o Pseudo-code
- Arithmetic
    - o Expressions
    - o Basic operators (+, -, x, /)
    - o Advanced operators: mod, floor, ceiling, etc.
- Concurrency
    - o Synchronization using broadcasting
- Conditional statements:
    - o Conditions: YES/NO questions
    - o Relational operators (=, <, >)
    - o Conditionals (IF)
    - o Conditionals (If-Else)
    - o Conditionals (nested IF)
    - o Boolean operators (and, or, not)
- Data structures – list
    - o List operations
    - o Using list as 2-D array
    - o List traversal
- Data types – basic
    - o Integers
- Data types – strings
    - o String operations (join, letter, length of)
- Events
- Looping (iteration)
    - o Looping - simple (repeat, forever)
    - o Looping - simple (for)

- o Looping - nested
        - o Looping - conditional (repeat until)
- Motion
        - o Motion - absolute
- Procedures
        - o Built-in
        - o User defined (custom)
        - o Simple
        - o With inputs
        - o With return value
- Program output
        - o Text
- Random numbers
- Recursion
- Sequence
- Sounds - playing sounds
- STAMP - creating images
- Stopping scripts
- User input
        - o Text
        - o Click buttons
        - o Keyboard events
        - o Mouse events
- Variables
        - o Simple
        - o Properties (built-in)
        - o Local/global scope
- XY Geometry

High Level Design:

This is where we take a step back from the computer, analyze the problem in our mind (and on a piece of paper if necessary), and break it down into multiple smaller ideas which can be programmed separately.

Let us take a look at the main screen of the game and try to point out the different pieces.

The following ideas come to mind at this point:
- To draw the 4x4 grid of squares we will use the STAMP command.
- We will have 16 sprites: 4 animal types each with 4 colors.
  - Each sprite will have a unique id telling us its type and color.
  - Each sprite will know (save in its private variables) its location in the grid.
- To represent the 4x4 grid, we will use a list L1 with 16 items.
- To represent the free queue, we will use a list L2 whose length would depend on how many are free.
- Manual play:
  - When an animal is clicked, depending on where it is (L1 or L2), appropriate action will be taken. Rules of the game will be checked before it is moved.
- Computer play:
  - We will "simulate" the clicks so that much of the logic can be re-used when the computer tries to solve the puzzle.

We will need the following information available to the entire program, and hence it is best kept in global variables.

Global variables:
Xorigin and Yorigin: northwest corner of the grid (used to calculate positions of other cells)
cellSize: size of each cell in the grid
Width: used for animal positioning in the "free queue" (to ensure all 16 of them can fit)
Glide time: time taken when each animal moves between the zoo and the free queue (we will make it a slider so that the user can change it)

Initial Set of Features:

Clearly it makes sense to start with the most basic features:
- Set up the zoo which can hold animals.
- When an animal is clicked it should respond appropriately.
- Create the initial random layout of animals inside the zoo.

This would be a good set of features using which the user can play the basic game.

Feature Idea # 1: The 4x4 zoo with animals
Draw a 4x4 grid of cells and display animals.

Design:

Step 1: The 4x4 board of squares

We can use a single square sprite and using STAMP to create this 4x4 grid. We will simply borrow an older program called "*Matrix-1*" (from the book "Practice CS Concepts with Snap") which provides just this functionality. This includes a "square" sprite that can create a 4x4 grid using STAMP.

Note: The *Matrix-1* program is available in the files provided with this book.

Step 2: The animals

There are 16 animals: of 4 kinds, each of 4 different colors. We need some way to give a unique ID for each animal: we could use 2 letters, one for the type (dog, dinosaur, etc.) and the other for the color (red, blue, etc.). For example, "a1" could mean animal "a" with color "1", d3 means animal "d" with color "3", etc. Let's assign these letters as below:

a: crab, b: dinosaur, c: dog, d: penguin
1: red, 2: blue, 3: yellow, 4: green

Thus, we will have 16 separate sprites and each will hold its ID in a private variable (myID).

Step 3: The zoo (4x4 grid) and placement of animals

We have already taken care of the 4x4 grid of squares. Now, we will figure out how to place the animals in this grid. We will use a 16-item list to represent the 4x4 board. The 16-item list would be one dimensional whereas the board is 2-D. We will calculate the row and column numbers from the cell number. For example, if the cell number is 7, its row would be 2 and column would be 3.

This list (let's call it L1) will contain the IDs of animals (e.g. a1, d2, etc.). If a cell is empty, it will contain 0.

As soon as the initial layout (which animal goes into which cell) is determined and saved in L1, each animal will look up its location in L1, calculate its row and column, and save them in its private variables "myrow" and "mycol". We will call this script "Enter zoo", whose algorithm is given below:

```
Algorithm Enter Zoo: (run by every animal sprite)
I = find my location in L1 (using the "index" command in Snap)
Calculate row and column from I.
Save them in private variables myrow and mycol.
Calculate x, y of my cell and move there.
```


Step 4: The free queue (where animals line up when they are free)

We will use another list, called L2, which will hold animals (i.e. their IDs) freed from the grid. Its length will vary as animals enter or leave it. L2's contents (i.e. the animals) will be displayed at the bottom of the screen, right to left. We will need to resize the animal sprites such that all 16 can fit on the screen.

Feature Idea # 2: Process the click

When an animal is clicked it should respond appropriately.

Design:

"Appropriately" means the following:
- If the animal is in the zoo, and if there is no one in front of it (i.e. to its right), and if its color or type matches with the last free animal in L2, it should move to L2.
- If the animal is in L2, and if there is no one behind it (i.e. to its left) it should move back to its original cell in the zoo.
- In all other cases, it should ignore the click.

It should be straightforward to design the algorithm for this. We notice that, a part of this algorithm takes place entirely in the backend (i.e. in L1 and L2), and part of it involves visible movements (gliding of sprites). Since the first part is common for all sprites, we will build it as a separate algorithm which can be shared among all animal sprites (as a custom block).

Part 1: Algorithm Process Click (common to all animal sprites, custom block):
Return value: 1 if animal should move from L1 to L2, 2 if animal should move from L1 to L2, 0 if no move.

Determine if it's in the grid or free.
- Use the "contains" operator to check if it's in the L2 list. If yes, the animal is free, else it is in the grid.

(A) If it's in the free row and is the last one in L2, it will be moved back to its position in the grid.

(B) If it's in the grid: all conditions below will be checked and the animal will be added to L2 and moved to the queue at screen bottom.

-   Verify there is no one ahead in the same row. (If there is someone, do nothing.)
```
Verify column=4 OR
Verify [row, column+1] is empty.
     Location in L1 = (row-1)*4 + column+1
     Verify item at this location is zero.
```
-   If L2 is not empty, verify color matches with color or type of the last item in L2.
```
If L2 is empty, go ahead with the move. OR
Get color and type of the last item in L2
Compare color and type of the last item in L2 with the clicked
animal, go ahead with the move.
```

Part 2: Algorithm "When Clicked" (each animal sprite will have its own copy):
```
Call "Process Click" (part 1 above) and get return value RetVal.
If RetVal = 1
Glide to end of L2 (calculate x, y using # of items in L2)
If RetVal = 2
Calculate x, y using myrow, mycol and glide to x,y
```

Feature Idea # 3: Puzzle layout
Create the initial layout of animals trapped inside the 4x4 zoo.

Design:
In order to get a different layout every time, we will use "random" distribution. Basically we will shuffle the 16-animal list L1. Instead of designing our own algorithm for this purpose, we will use an existing one: Donald Knuth's shuffle algorithm as described below:

```
L: list of N items
For i from 0 to N-2 do:
     j = random integer such that i <= j < N
     Exchange items L[i+1] and L[j+1]
```

We will add a button sprite called "New game" that will allow the user to create a new layout and play another round of the puzzle. This button will just send a broadcast to let everyone (including the above script) to know that they should get ready for a new game.

Save version 1:

Congratulations! You have completed all the features attempted so far. Compare your program with my program in the file below.

Solution: zoo-escape-1.xml

Next Set of Features:

Now it makes sense to tackle the following features:
- Provide a way for the computer to solve the puzzle.
- Using the 'h' key the user should be able to view instructions and rules of the game.

Feature Idea # 4: Computer solves puzzle

Create an approach by which the program can solve the puzzle, i.e. create a sequence of moves to free all animals.

Design:

We will use the "exhaustive search" idea (also known as the "Brute force" approach) to systematically try out all possible moves until a solution is found.

Step 1: Allow the computer to "simulate" a click.

Since the game is run by clicking on animals (either in the grid or in the free list), we should first figure out a way to simulate this click. This is really quite straightforward. Right now each animal has a "When I am clicked" script. We will change it to be invoked by a broadcast message. For instance, for animal "a1" its script will be invoked by "When I receive a1-clicked".

All animal scripts will be thus modified. Clearly this would not affect the "manual play" behavior since "When I am clicked" will simply send the appropriate broadcast message.

But, now we have a way to simulate a click. We just need to send the appropriate broadcast message to create the illusion that some animal was clicked.

The advantage of simulating clicks is that the computer doesn't have worry about checking game rules etc. because all that logic is already in place in the click scripts. Even invalid clicks would be taken care of!

Step 2: Write the exhaustive search algorithm to find a solution.

This is how exhaustive search works: we scan the list L1 from the beginning and look for a "candidate" animal, i.e. an animal that can be moved to L2. Then we simulate a click on it. We repeat these steps. If no animal can be found in L1, we undo the previous move, i.e. we send the last freed animal back to the zoo by simulating a click on it. Then we once again scan L1 for a "candidate" animal, but from the place where the "undo" animal returned.

Every time the search for a "candidate" animal succeeds, we reset the search location to the beginning of L1.

We essentially repeat this process until either L1 becomes empty (which means success), or L2 becomes empty (which means there is no solution).

Here is the algorithm:
```
Location N = 1
Repeat until L2 has 16 animals:
```

Search for candidate animal:
```
Scan L1 from N for an animal that can be moved (which has no animal in
front)
Simulate click
Continue this scan until click succeeds (meaning all rules for the
move are satisfied) OR until no candidate animal is found in L1
```

After search:
```
If success:
        Reset N = 1
Else
        If L2 is empty
                Declare "No solution to this puzzle"
```

```
            Stop
        Else
                Get grid location of last animal in L2.
                    (See note on "Get grid location" below)
                N = location of moved animal + 1
                Move last animal in L2 back to grid (simulate click)
                Go back to "search for candidate animal" above
        End if
End if
End repeat
```

How to get grid location of the last animal in L2:
Snap allows a sprite to look up private variables of other sprites via the following operator in the "Sensing" palette:

If you insert the sprite name in the second input of this operator, the first drop-down list shows names of that sprite's private variables also. In our program, every animal sprite has "myrow" and "mycol" as private variables that can thus be accessed through this operator. See the example below:

Using this operator, we can find out the grid location (i.e. row and column) of any animal.

Finally, we will invoke this option (of computer solving the puzzle) when user presses the "s" key. We could have created a button for this, but, that would be too tempting for a lazy user! □

Important note: While trying to solve the puzzle, we will first undo all the manual moves made by the user thus far. This is necessary because otherwise the "search space" of the brute-force approach will be limited. For example, imagine that the user started with the animal in row=4, column=4 and the actual solution requires some previous animal. The brute-force algorithm above will end up sending all free animals back to the zoo, and giving up as soon as the animal in row=4, column=4 is sent back, concluding that "there is no solution" because L2 would be empty then.

Feature Idea # 5: Add help screen
Using the 'h' key the user should be able to view instructions and rules of the game.

Design:
We can split the playing instructions and rules of the game on two separate screens (costumes) and use a single sprite which shows up when 'h' is pressed. The user can then press another key to see the second costume (showing game rules).

While we are at it, we will also add some background music that can be played (after pressing SPACE key) when the computer is trying to find the solution (which can go on for a while).

Save version 2:
Congratulations! You have completed all the features listed so far. Compare your program with my program in the file below.

Solution: zoo-escape-2.xml

Final Set of Features:
Now let us wrap things up by adding the following features:
-   Provide the option to disable (hide) actual moves in the "auto" mode to save some time.
-   Earlier, we used the approach of creating a random layout. Not all such layouts lead to a solution. Use an approach that always creates a solvable puzzle layout.
-   This new approach to get puzzle layouts means we don't need the "brute force method" to find a solution. Modify the approach to suit our modified approach to design layouts.

Feature Idea # 6: Hide moves

Provide the option to hide trial moves in the "auto" mode.

Design:

You must have noticed in the previous version that the brute force approach can take a long time to find the solution since there can potentially be lots and lots of legal moves. This time is spent in two activities: one is running through the algorithm scanning L1 for legal moves, and the other is actually moving (gliding) the animals back and forth between the grid and the freedom queue. As we know, a lot of the moves are just trial moves. We could save some time if we prevent the "glides" of the trial moves.

Well, there is no easy way to distinguish between a good move and a trial move. Instead, what we can do is prevent all glides and just work on finding the solution, i.e. finding the sequence of animals which when clicked would result in solving the puzzle. Once we find this sequence, then we can turn on gliding and show just the 16 good moves.

We will have a global variable to turn off the glides, so that, the user can decide (by setting this variable to True or False) whether they want to see the algorithm in action on the screen or just see the final solution. (Let's call this variable "backendOnly"; if it is True glides are disabled.)

The glides are in each animal sprite's click script. We use the "Process Click" algorithm which is common to all sprites before the glides. Depending on its return value (1 or 2) the direction of the glide is determined. If "Process Click" returns 0, the animal does nothing. We will use this trick to disable the glides. "Process Click" will check the value of "backendOnly" to decide when to return 0.

Actual setting of this global variable can be done from the "find solution" algorithm to ensure glides are disabled before we start the recursive search. When the search is over, the solution would be sitting in L2. We can then copy it to another list, say "solution", empty L2, and then play the "solution" visually so the user can see the 16 good moves.

Here is the outline of how we can accomplish "hiding" of the glides:

```
<Un-do all user manual moves>
```

```
If backendOnly = True
      Make a temporary copy of L1 in tempL1
End if
<Run the find solution algorithm>
If backendOnly = True
      Copy L2 to Solution
      Empty L2
      Copy tempL1 back to L1
      backendOnly = False
      For each item in Solution
            Simulate a click on item
      End for
End if
```

Feature Idea # 7: Solvable puzzle layout

Earlier, we used the approach of creating a random layout. Not all such layouts lead to a solution. Use an approach that will always create a solvable puzzle layout.

Design:

As mentioned, our earlier approach of using a random layout does not always lead to a solution. Here is one such random layout that is unsolvable:

Trying to solve a potentially unsolvable puzzle can indeed be frustrating for the user. So, we need a better way to create puzzle layouts. One idea is to reverse-engineer, that is, create a solution first and then create a layout that would lead to that solution.

As you know, the "solution" is what gets created in L2 when the puzzle is fully solved. It is a sequence of 16 animals which follows the game rules. Can we create random sequences that can qualify as valid "solutions"?

Absolutely! All we have to do is start with a random animal A1 and then pick another animal A2 to follow it such that A2 is either of the same color or type as A1. Next, we pick another animal A3 to follow A2 the same way, and so on. The approach is clearly repeatable or recursive. We will basically need two lists: "solution" which gets built up by adding one animal at a time, and "free animals" which supplies these animals (should be shuffled so that every time we get a different solution).

Here is the algorithm of step 1 of the overall algorithm to build a puzzle layout:

Algorithm "Add Free Animal" (brute-force recursive approach):
Initial call: Add Free Animal (L, Animals) where L contains one animal and Animals is a shuffled list of remaining 15 animals.

```
If Animals is empty return Success (because all animals have been
used)
tempL = list of candidate animals from Animals that fit the last
animal in L (use algorithm "Get Candidates" below)
For each animal A in tempL
        Move A from Animals to L
        Recurse with (L, Animals)
        If return code = Success, return Success
        else
                Move A from L to Animals (undo)
                Continue with For loop (try the next animal in tempL)
        End if
End for
Return Fail
```

Step 2 is to take the "solution" list and remove animals from it (from the tail) and place them in the grid (L1) from left to right. We will pick each new cell randomly such that:
1. It is always to the right of an already filled cell or is the 1st in its row.
2. The two neighbors obey the rule that their color or type matches.

Here is the algorithm of this step 2.

Algorithm Create Layout:
Initial call with (Solution, Layout) where Solution is the list created in step 1 above, and Layout is the grid originally filled with 16 zeros.

```
Repeat until Solution is empty:
     Remove the last item A in Solution
     Find a random row R in Layout that is not full
     Place A at the end of R
End repeat
```

Algorithm for the utility "Get Candidates" (used in Step 1 above):
We basically look for animals for which either the color or type matches with the target animal.

Input: Animals: list of animals, A: target animal with whom to match
Steps:
```
Candidates = []
For each animal in Animals
     If color of animal = color of A OR type of animal = type of A
          Add animal to Candidates
     End if
End for
Return Candidates
```

Feature Idea # 8: Computer solves puzzle
Earlier, we used the brute force method to find a solution. Modify the approach to suit our modified approach to design layouts.

Design:
Since we are creating the layouts ourselves (and not using random layouts) we already know the solution. (See Step 1 of Feature "Solvable puzzle layout" above). Now, we just need to "play" this solution if user asks the computer to solve the puzzle.

As before we will undo all moves made by the user first and then simulate clicks on each animal in the "solution" list.

Save version final:

Congratulations! You have completed all the features of the game. Compare your program with my program at the file or link below.

Solution: zoo-escape-final.xml

Berkeley Snap site: Zoo escape
(`https://snap.berkeley.edu/snap/snap.html#present:Username=abjoshi&ProjectName =zoo-escape-final`)

How to run the program:
1. Click green flag or "New Game" to start playing. Press 'h' to see help.
2. Play the game yourself by clicking on the animals. Your aim is to free all animals from the zoo (the grid).
3. Press "s" any time to let the computer try to solve the puzzle.

Project 9: Zork – monsters in dungeon

Creativity is the process by which men and women play or often struggle with chaos and transform it into something that has taken on beauty and purpose.
– Unknown

Program description

Zork is an interactive game of monsters in the dungeon. We will write a simplified version of the original Zork game developed in the 1970s at MIT. (See https://en.wikipedia.org/wiki/Zork for more information.) In this game, there is a multi-story dungeon in which each floor contains multiple rooms. The gamer is initially put into some random room (where exactly in the dungeon they don't know) and they need to find a way to the room that contains the 'grand prize'. Since the user has no idea where they are, they need to use the available commands to find the way. On their way, they may have to fight monsters, grab swords and magic stones, and move up or down the dungeon. See the game specification below to understand all the rules.

Program Specification:

This game takes place in a 3-story dungeon, each story containing 7 rooms. The game provides these commands: left, right, up, down, grab, fight, help, quit, and new. These commands are explained below. The goal of the game is to collect the 'grand prize' guarded by the boss monster.

At the start of the game, the user is placed randomly in one of the empty rooms. The program UI should reveal the structure of the dungeon as it unfolds through exploration.

Movement

The user can use 'left' and 'right' commands to move to the left or right room. If there is no room in that direction, the game should report this. The user can also use 'up' and 'down' to move upstairs or downstairs if the room contains the required staircase.

Contents of rooms

A room can contain: a sword, a monster, a boss monster, grand prize, magic stones, up-stairs, down-stairs or nothing. The game informs the user of the contents of the current room after every command. The user can 'grab' swords or magic stones if they walk into a room with them. The sword or stones are no longer in the room once grabbed.

Monsters

There should be three regular monsters placed throughout the game. The user must use a sword to defeat a monster using the 'fight' command. The sword and monster disappear after fighting. If they have no sword, the user can run away in the direction from which they came. If the user fights without a sword, they will be defeated and the game will end. If they try to walk past a monster, they will be killed and the game will end. There should be a boss monster in the room next to the room that contains the grand prize. A sword and magic stones are required to defeat the boss monster.

User assets

These are items that the user grabs along the way. A maximum of three items can be held at a time.

Win/Lose

The game is won when the player grabs the grand prize. The game is lost if the user fights a monster without a sword, fights the boss monster without a sword and stones, or tries to move past a monster. There may be situations when the game is unwinnable because of the way the dungeon is set up, in which case the user can start a new game.

Explore the game:

If you want to play with my final program to get a feel for this game, click the Snap link specified at the end of the chapter. Try not to peek at the scripts yet, since we want to design them ourselves below. We will implement two versions of this game: (1) A simple version in which the game logic is implemented but the graphical user interface is mostly non-existent, and (2) A fully functional graphical version. The following image shows a snapshot of the final working version of the game:

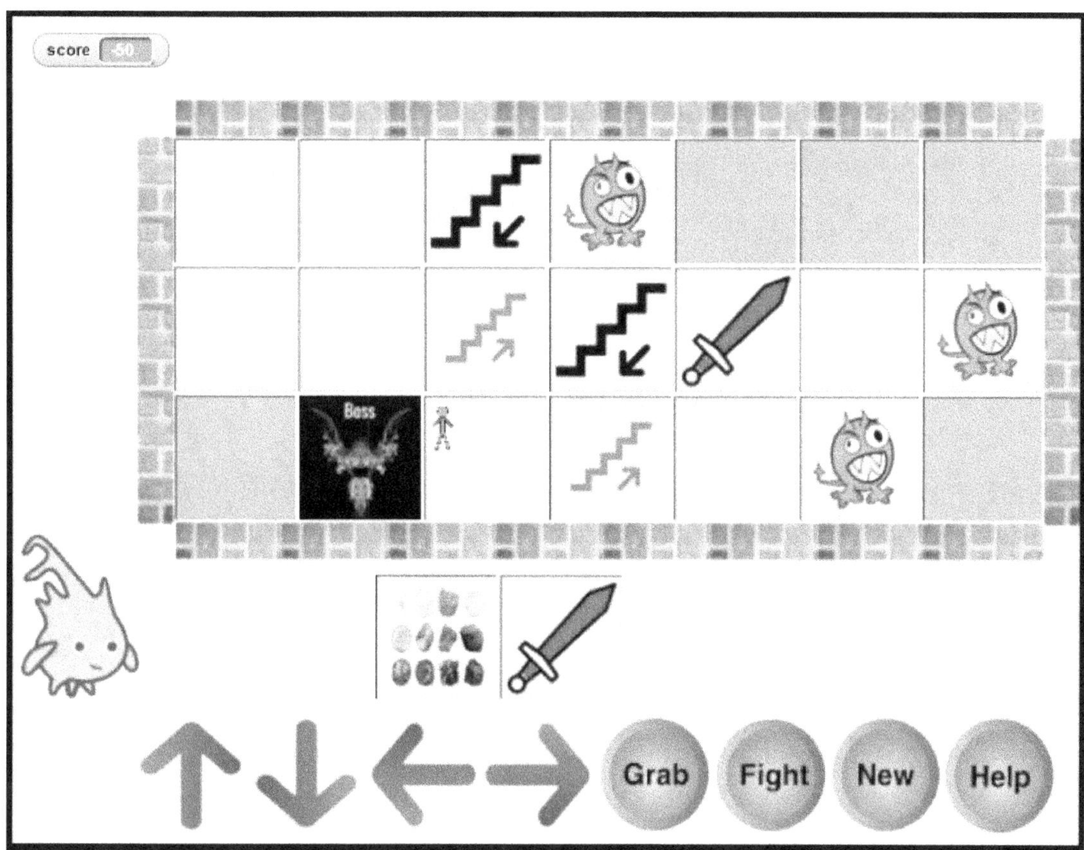

Steps to run the program:

1. Click the Green flag. All game data will be reset. Click Help to understand game rules.
2. The initial "known" layout of just the current room will be shown.
3. Play the game by clicking the available commands.
4. The known structure of the dungeon and user assets are shown after every command.
5. Click "New" to play with a new dungeon if you are stuck or when the game is over.

Snap and CS Concepts Used

When we design this program, we will make use of the following Snap and CS concepts. Learn these concepts if you don't know them before proceeding further.

- Algorithms
    - Designing new algorithms
- Arithmetic
    - Expressions
    - Basic operators (+, -, x, /)
    - Advanced operators: mod, floor, etc.
- Concurrency:
    - Synchronization using broadcasting
- Conditional statements:
    - Conditions: YES/NO questions
    - Relational operators (=, <, >)
    - Conditionals (IF)
    - Conditionals (If-Else)
    - Conditionals (nested IF)
    - Boolean operators (and, or, not)
- Data structures – list
    - List operations: add, insert, replace, remove, scanning
    - Using list as 2-D array
    - Advanced list processing
- Data types – basic
    - Integers
- Data types – strings
    - String operations
- Looping (iteration)
    - Looping - simple (repeat, for)
    - Looping - nested
    - Looping - conditional (repeat until)
- OOP
    - Clones
- Pen Art
    - Stamp
- Procedures

- o   User defined (custom)
- o   Procedures with parameters and return value
- Program output
  - o   Text
  - o   GUI (sprites)
- Random numbers
- Sequence
- User input
  - o   Text
  - o   Click buttons
- User interface elements
  - o   Sprites and costumes
  - o   Buttons
  - o   Clones
- Variables
  - o   Simple
  - o   Local/global scope
  - o   Script variables

High Level Design

Although we want to finally design the game with the full graphical interface shown above, we will first design a version with minimal graphical elements. But, clearly, most of the logic of the game would be very similar for the two versions.

Let us think about how we will go about designing this backend logic.

A big part of this game's appeal is mystery: i.e. the user does not know beforehand how the dungeon is laid out. They know it is a 3-story structure with each floor containing 7 rooms. But, which room contains what is left to exploration. That means, we will need a **procedure to set up the dungeon** such that every time it looks different. We will explore it in the algorithm called "Setup Dungeon" later below.

The other big part of the game is simply enforcing the various rules. We can do this by having separate algorithms for each user command. So, for example, the "up" command would move the user to the upper floor if the current room contains stairs to go up.

Another interesting and important aspect of the program is the way the dungeon reveals itself to the user as they explore it. In fact, their success depends on this evolving knowledge. The program will need to use separate data structures to keep track of this "user view", and also have algorithms to update this view as the user makes discoveries about the dungeon. We will cover all this stuff in a separate feature idea called "User view of the dungeon".

Once we properly design our main data structures to manage the various pieces of information, such as, the dungeon itself, user assets, etc., we can move on to the task of designing various algorithms as we tackle the features one by one.

As usual, we will design the backend (the logic of the game) and the frontend (code that handles user interaction) separately and connect them at appropriate places.

Let us first design the data structures (i.e. data types and variables that will hold all the important information).

Data structures:
- The dungeon: 3 stories with 7 rooms each
  - A list called "dungeon" containing 3 sub-lists, each sub-list containing 7 rooms
  - Each room is shown by its content: 'sword', 'monster', 'boss monster', 'magic stones', 'up-stairs', 'down-stairs', 'grand prize', 'nothing', or 'unknown'
- User assets: the items that the user collects and uses in the dungeon
  - A list called "userAssets" containing 3 items max: each item can be 'sword', 'magic stones', or 'grand prize'
- User location in the dungeon: the program needs to track where the user is (although the user does not know)
  - Two integers "userFloor" (can be 1 thru 3) and "userRoom" (can be 1 thru 7)

Front-end:

In the first version, the front-end is quite simple: we will just display the above data structures (lists and other variables) to track what is going on in the game, and use the "ask" command to get user input. Note that Snap allows us to display 2-D lists (i.e. lists that contain lists, like our dungeon) in a table format which is much easier to understand.

Global data:

We will maintain the following data as global variables:
- The dungeon (2-D list)
- User assets (list)
- Score (integer)
- User location (2 integers)

Feature Idea # 1: The movement commands

Implement the rules for these commands: right, left, up, down

Design:

For the sake of simplicity, we will assume that the dungeon is already set up (we will manually set up the "dungeon" list). The user is in some room that may or may not contain anything.

And now we just need to move the user through the dungeon using one of the motion commands. The algorithms for each of these commands derive easily from the rules that we know from the game specification. (Read the section "Specification" above.)

Please note that after each of these movements, we need to update the user's view of the dungeon. We will learn how to do this in a separate feature later. For now, we will just "call" that step in each of the algorithms below.

The "left" and "right" commands also check if you are "walking over" a monster. For this purpose, we will maintain a variable called prevCommand (previous command) which keeps a record of the previous command.

Algorithm command "Right"
Given: dungeon, user location (user floor and user room)
Steps:
If there is monster in the current room AND user is walking over (i.e.
user came to this room from the left)
        Declare that user loses and game is over
Else
        If there is room to the right
                Increment User room by 1
                Update user view of the dungeon
        Else
                Inform user there is no room to the right
        End if
End if

Algorithm command "Left"
Given: dungeon, user location (user floor and user room)
Steps:
If there is monster in the current room AND user is walking over (i.e.
user came to this room from the right)
        Declare that user loses and game is over
Else
        If there is room to the left
                Decrement User room by 1
                Update user view of the dungeon
        Else
                Inform user there is no room to the left
        End if
End if

Algorithm command "Up"
Given: dungeon, user location (user floor and user room)
If current room contains "up-stairs"
        Increment User floor by 1
        Update user view of the dungeon
Else
        Inform user there is no way to go up
End if

Algorithm command "Down"
Given: dungeon, user location (user floor and user room)
If current room contains "down-stairs"
        Decrement User floor by 1
        Update user view of the dungeon
Else
        Inform user there is no way to go down
End if

Feature Idea # 2: The action commands

Implement the rules for these commands: grab and fight.

Design:

The user is in some room that may or may not contain anything. And now we need to let the user run one of the action commands. The algorithms for each of these commands derive easily from the rules that we know from the game specification. (Read the section "Specification" above.)

Please note that after each of these actions, we need to update the user's view of the dungeon. As before, we will just "call" that step in each of the algorithms below.

```
Algorithm command "grab"
Given: content of the current room
Steps:
If content is the grand prize
     If boss monster has already been slain (we will use a variable
     to save this event)
          Declare victory and game is over
     Else
          Inform user that boss monster needs to be slain first
     End if
Else if content is sword or magic stones
     If user already has 3 assets
          Inform user that they cannot grab any more assets
     Else
          Move the asset from the room to user's asset list
          Update user view of the dungeon
     End if
End if
```

```
Algorithm command "fight"
Given: content of the current room
Steps:
If content is neither monster nor boss monster
     Inform the user there is no one to fight
     Return
End if
If content is monster
     If user has a sword
          Declare monster has been slain
          Remove monster and sword
          Update user view of the dungeon
```

```
        Else
                Declare user is dead and game over
        End if
End if
If content is boss monster
        If user has both sword and magic stones
                Declare boss monster has been slain
                Remove boss monster, sword, and magic stones
                Update user view of the dungeon
        Else
                Declare user is dead and game over
        End if
End if
```

Feature Idea # 3: Play the game

Now that we have all the basic commands in place, we should be able to play the game.

Design:

We just need a loop in which the user can enter commands (using the "ask" command) which the program will run and displays results. Since we don't yet have a "user view" of the dungeon, for now, we will just watch the entire dungeon as it is after every command. (Remember, in the final game the user needs to discover the dungeon.) We will also add a "quit" command.

Save as Program Version 1

Congratulations! You have completed the most basic features listed above. Compare your program with my program in the file below.

File: zork-0.xml

How to play the game:

1. Click the Green flag. All game data will be reset.
2. The entire dungeon is visible in a table format.
3. Play the game by entering the available commands.

Feature Idea # 4: Maintain user view

As the user explores the dungeon their knowledge of its structure evolves. Maintain this "user view" of the dungeon and show it to the user after every command.

Design:

The user's ability to navigate the dungeon to maximize their score and ultimately win depends on their knowledge of the dungeon. Initially, they only know that they are in a room containing nothing. They also know that the dungeon is 3-story and each floor contains seven rooms. The "user view" would thus be similar to the "dungeon" except that it grows from one room and one floor into the full 7-room 3-floor structure.

Step 1: Create data structures to hold and maintain this user view.

We will add the following new global variables to track the "user view".
viewDungeon: list of lists (similar to dungeon)
viewRoom and viewFloor: integers telling which room and floor in viewDungeon the user is currently occupying

Step 2: Create algorithms to update the view as the user explores the dungeon.

After every movement command, user's knowledge of the dungeon improves. Here are some examples:

- After every successful "right" or "left" command they discover an additional room.
- If "right" or "left" fails, they know they are at the right or left edge of the floor. They can deduce that the remaining unexplored rooms of the current floor, if any, must be at the opposite end.

After every action command, user's knowledge of the dungeon does not change, but the room contents may change.

Let's put all these inferences into an algorithm.

Algorithm Update User View

Purpose: Based on the command just executed, update the user view of
the dungeon.
Given: (1) name of command just executed, (2) content of the new room
(where user is after running the command), (3) did the command succeed
Steps:
If command was "left"
        If it did not succeed (there are no more rooms to the left)
                Add extra rooms (containing 'unknown' content) at the
                right end of all floors of "user view"
        Else
                If user is in the leftmost room of "user view"
                    Add 1 room at the left end of all floors (user view)
                End if
                Set the content of this room (in the view) with the actual
                content
        End if
End if
If command was "right"
        If it did not succeed (there are no more rooms to the right)
                Add extra rooms (containing 'unknown' content) at the left
                end of all floors of "user view"
        Else
                If user is in the rightmost room of "user view"
                    Add 1 room at the right end of all floors
                End if
                Set the content of this room (in the view) with the actual
                content
        End if
End if
If command was "down" AND user is in the lowermost floor of "user
view"
        Add a new floor below with the same # of rooms as the current
        floor; mark their content as "unknown"
End if
If command was "up" AND user is in the uppermost floor of "user view"
        Add a new floor above with the same # of rooms as the current
        floor; mark their content as "unknown"
End if
If command was "grab" or "fight" and was successful
        Just remove the content of the current room of "user view"
End if

<u>Step 3</u>: Display to the user the latest view of the dungeon after every command.

The "viewDungeon" list contains the view of the dungeon floor by floor. We can simply display this list in a table format. In addition, the viewRoom and viewFloor varibles will tell us the current location of the user in the view dungeon.

Feature Idea # 5: Game setup

So far we have been using a manually created dungeon. Write a procedure to automatically create a new dungeon. As mentioned earlier, this feature is important because it takes care of the mystery aspect of the dungeon. Every time the user runs the game, the dungeon structure, i.e. the content of various rooms should be different and the user should also be placed in a different location.

Add a new command to the game called 'new' which will set up a new dungeon and restart the game.

Design:

Here are the rules for the dungeon setup:
- There must be at least 3 monsters total (ideally one on each floor), and one and only one 'boss monster'.
- There must be one and only one 'grand prize'.
- 'boss monster' and 'grand prize' rooms must be next to each other.
- The staircases must go in pairs: for example, if stairs going down from floor 3 are in room 4, the stairs going up from floor 2 must also be in room 4.
- Place 3 swords and 2 'magic stones' spread throughout the dungeon.

Since the boss monster and prize must go together, we will place them first. The stairs can go next because they also have the constraint of going in pairs. Monsters, swords, magic stones, and the user can then be placed in the remaining available rooms.

Here is the algorithm:

```
Algorithm Setup new dungeon
Given: dungeon (3 element list with each element containing 7 items)
Steps:
Store 'nothing' in all rooms of the dungeon.
```

```
Create a list 'rooms' that shows all unused rooms, initially all 1
thru 21. Update this list every time a room is allocated below.
Place the 'grand prize':
     Pick at random a floor and a room on it
     Save 'grand prize'
Place the 'boss monster' in the room next to grand prize
Place the stairs:
     For each of the bottom 2 floors:
          Find an empty room such that the room above it is also
          empty
          Save 'up-stairs' and 'down-stairs' in these 2 rooms
     End for
Place monsters:
     For each of the 3 floors:
          Find an empty room and save 'monster'
     End for
Place swords:
     Repeat 3 times:
     Pick at random an empty anywhere in the dungeon
     Save 'sword'
End repeat
Place magic stones:
     Repeat 2 times:
          Pick at random an empty room anywhere in the dungeon
          Save 'magic stones'
     End repeat
Place the user:
     Pick at random an empty room anywhere in the dungeon
     Save user location (floor and room)
```

Save this version

Congratulations! You have completed all the logic of the game. Compare your
program with my program in the file below.

File: zork-1.xml

How to play the game:

1. Click the Green flag. All game data will be reset.
2. "viewDungeon" list shows the initial "known" layout of just the current room.
3. Play the game by entering the available commands.
4. The known structure of the dungeon and user assets are shown after every
   command.

GUI Version: Overview

In this version, we will convert the simple user interface into a shiny graphical user interface that we saw at the start of this document. Here it is once again, with more details.

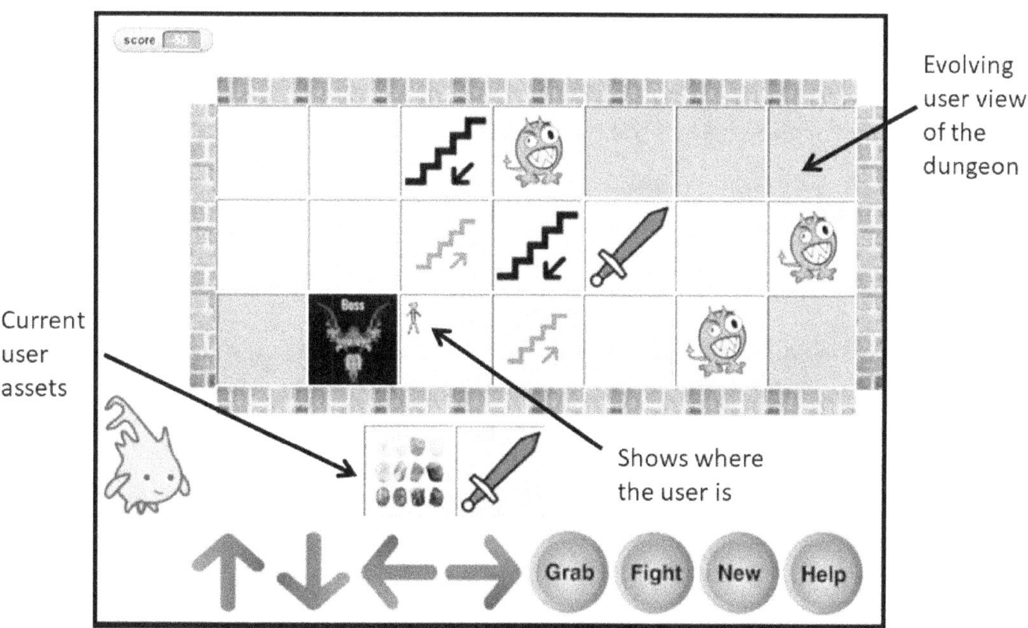

Since we already have most of the game logic in place, we only need to figure out how to replace the current interface with an interface where the latest "user view" of the dungeon is always visible and user input comes via clicks.

Feature Idea # 6: Setup the GUI

Create the layout of all the required GUI elements.

Design:

Front-end components:

Let us list the information that we must present to the user:
- The evolving view of the dungeon (this can be shown as a grid that can grow from 1 box to 3 rows x 7 columns)

- User's current assets (3 images max)
- Message area to show errors or other helpful messages
- Score

In addition, we will need to provide click-buttons for the user to enter all available commands.

Let us now design the display to properly present all these difference pieces. We will use a grid format for the view of the dungeon.

GUI layout:

The dungeon:
- Brick wall on all 4 sides (purely for aesthetic purposes): we could use horizontal and vertical brick images and use the "stamp" feature to create the walls high and wide enough to contain the dungeon
- The 3x7 dungeon: we will use a "cell" sprite to represent a single room and clone it to all visible rooms. (More below)

User assets:
- 3 images: a single sprite with costumes for sword, magic stones and prize, use cloning to display multiple assets

Command buttons:
- Sprites for "Help" and other game commands (7 total)

Message area:
- We will use a sprite to "say" the messages

Score:
- Show the "score" variable

Contents of the dungeon:
We will need a lot of images most of which will be of identical dimensions (80x80 to be precise) to fit in each room of the dungeon. We will use a single sprite called "cell" that

will have costumes to show all possible contents of a dungeon room: sword, up-stairs, down-stairs, magic stones, monster, boss monster, grand prize, and 'unknown' (when the user does not know what's in a room). We will then use "clones" to display the visible dungeon.

Feature Idea # 7: Setup the Click buttons
Create the buttons for user to click to enter commands.

Design:
Since we already have a loop in the backend logic to process user commands, we can just have each click button send a broadcast message to this loop. We could use a variable (called "command") to let the script know which button was clicked. Subsequent work would be the same as before.

Feature Idea # 8: Display the view dungeon and user assets
As the user discovers new rooms of the dungeon they start appearing on the display. Also display the assets user currently possesses.

Design:

**Step 1**: Display the initial and updated user view.

Initially, the user sees only one room. But, where should we show this room? The user is not supposed to know which floor and which room of that floor it is supposed to be. To keep matters simple, we will show this room in the bottom-left corner of the grid – although it DOES NOT mean that the room is the 1st room on the 1st floor of the actual dungeon. If the user goes 'left' a room is added to the left, i.e. the view would now show two rooms in the bottom-left corner. If another 'left' fails (because there is no room) the view would add 5 rooms to the right showing 'unknown' content. The view would now show the entire 1st floor, although, once again, that does not mean the user is on the first floor of the actual dungeon.

This approach makes it easy for us to display the "user view". We just take the "viewDungeon" list and display it anchored to the bottom-left corner of the grid. Thus, if "viewDungeon" contains 2 sub-lists with 3 items each, we would display a 2x3 grid of rooms (with their contents) in the bottom-left corner.

To keep things simple, we will use the cloning feature to show all visible rooms of the dungeon. Based on the content of "viewDungeon" each clone would know where to show up and what costume to show. For instance, if the room is empty, the clone would use the "nothing" costume.

Here is the algorithm to display the "view dungeon":

```
For each floor in view dungeon:
    For each room in view dungeon:
        Switch costume to the "content" of the room
        Create clone
        Position for the next room
    End for
    Position for the next floor
End for
```

The script to display user assets would be similar.

***Step 2**: Indicate the current user position.*

We will use a tiny "user" image and overlay it on top of the cell that indicates the current user location. This sprite will position itself in the left-upper corner of the room currently occupied by the user (see the picture above). When we update the user view, we will simply move this stick figure to the new user position.

Feature Idea # 9: Add the 'help' command
Allow the user to see game instructions using the help command.

Design:
This is a simple matter of adding the command in our existing list and having a separate sprite to display the help.

Save the final GUI version

Congratulations! You have completed all features of the game for the GUI version. Compare your program with my program in the file below.

File: zork-2.xml

How to play the game:

1. Click the Green flag. All game data will be reset. Click Help to understand game rules.
2. The initial "known" layout of just the current room will be shown.
3. Play the game by clicking the available commands.
4. The known structure of the dungeon and user assets are shown after every command.
5. Click "New" to play with a new dungeon if you are stuck or when the game is over.

Advanced features

There are a few improvements we can make to this game:

(1) One of the game rules dictates that user can exit (escape) a room containing a monster by leaving the way they entered that room. We have currently implemented this rule by simply comparing current command with the previous command ("prevCommand"). This works only if the user exits right away, e.g. "right" followed by "left". What if the user clicks help/grab/up/down before exiting? Fix this problem.

(2) The game works through click buttons. Allow users also to use keys, e.g. "up arrow" for up, "g" for grab, "left arrow" for left, and so on.

(3) We display the entire view dungeon (by deleting all clones and showing them again) every time a command is entered. As you must have noticed this causes quite a flicker in the display. Make this more efficient: for example, when the user simply moves through the known area of the dungeon, there is no need to refresh the view.

Design:

I will leave the design and implementation of these features to you. But, here are hints for each of these features:

(1) This is a matter of using the "prevCommand" variable only for movement commands.

(2) This is just a matter of duplicating scripts for the event "When key pressed".

(3) Since what we display is "viewDungeon" we need to refresh only if this data structure changes. You could have a new variable that would indicate if "viewDungeon" is modified (either by adding new rooms or by modifying the content of any of the rooms). The GUI code would then look at this variable to decide whether to refresh the entire view or just update the position of the user stick figure.

You can see my scripts for these features in the file below.

Save the advanced version

Congratulations! You have completed all the advanced features of the game. Compare your program with my program in the file below.

File: zork-final.xml
Berkeley website: Zork final
(https://snap.berkeley.edu/snapsource/snap.html#present:Username=abjoshi&Proje
ctName=zork-final)

 | *Adventures in Snap Programming*

Project 10: Solo Chess

"Yes, the solution seems to work, it appears to be correct; but how is it possible to invent such a solution? … How could I invent or discover such things by myself?"
– George Polya

Program description

This program implements a popular board game that purports to "train" young minds for the game of chess. It is a one-player game which basically focuses on how the chess pieces are moved on the board. The following section describes how the game is played.

How the game is played:

- Use a 4x4 chess board (instead of the standard 8x8)
- Use only 2 pieces each of bishop, knight, pawn, queen, and rook. Color doesn't matter.
- The game begins with an initial layout with some of these pieces already laid out in some fashion. (In the real board game, a card shows the layout.)
- Start playing with any piece:
    - Rule 1: Every move must kill another piece (using usual Chess rules)
    - Rule 2: Every move may use a different piece
    - Rule 3: When only 1 piece is left on the board, the game is over (you win!)
- The challenge is thus to play (without violating the above rules) until only 1 piece is left.

Here is an example:

This image indicates one possible initial board layout:

The following moves indicate how the game can be finished:

Queen takes rook   Knight takes queen   Knight takes pawn

Explore the game:

If you want to play with my final program to get a feel for this game, click the link given at the end of the chapter. Try not to peek at the scripts yet, since we want to design them ourselves below.

1. Click the "Green flag". Read help and then click to continue.
2. Pick one of the levels of expertise. The initial layout will be shown.
3. Play the game by following the instructions on the left side. Click "Undo" to retract a move. You can undo multiple times.
4. Press "s" any time to make the computer play the game.

Snap and CS Concepts Used

When we design this program, we will make use of the following Snap and CS concepts. Learn these concepts if you don't know them before proceeding further.

- Arithmetic
  - o Expressions
  - o Basic operators (+, -, x, /)
  - o Advanced operators: mod, floor, ceiling, etc.
- Concurrency
  - o Synchronization using broadcasting
- Conditional statements:
  - o Conditions: YES/NO questions
  - o Relational operators (<, >, =)
  - o Conditionals (IF)
  - o Conditionals (If-Else)
  - o Conditionals (Wait until)
  - o Conditionals (nested IF)
  - o Boolean operators (and, or, not)
- Data structures – list
  - o List operations
  - o Using list as 2-D array
- Data types – basic
  - o Integers
- Data types – strings
  - o String operations (join, split)

- o String traversal
- Divide and conquer (program design technique)
- Events
- Looping (iteration)
  - o Looping - simple (repeat, forever)
  - o Looping - nested
- Motion
  - o Motion - absolute
- OOP
  - o Clones
- Procedures
  - o Built-in
  - o User defined (custom)
  - o Simple
  - o With inputs and return value
- Program output
  - o Text
- Recursion
- Sequence
- STAMP - creating images
- User input
  - o Click buttons
- Variables
  - o Simple
  - o Properties (built-in)
  - o Local/global scope
- XY Geometry

High Level Design

Let us take a quick look at the main screen of my program and then consider how the various features of this program can be separated out as distinct pieces.

As usual, we have the front-end that interacts with the user, and the back-end that performs all game functions.

Front-end components:
- 4x4 chess-board:
    - Shows the current layout
    - When the user clicks on a chess piece, informs the backend which cell was clicked
- 10 chess pieces (2 each of rook, bishop, pawn, queen, knight)
    - If a cell contains a chess piece, its image is shown on top of the cell
- Click button for "Undo"

For the frontend, we can simply borrow an older program called "*Chessboard*" (from the book "Practice CS Concepts with Snap") which provides just this functionality. Since blank cells do not need to be click-sensitive, we can use stamping to draw the board and show chess pieces on top of them using cloning.

Note: The *Chessboard* program is available in the files provided with this book.

Back-end components:

- 4x4 layout of the board: list of 16 letters: 0 for empty, Q, B, K, R, P for the chess pieces
    - The initial layout is obtained from somewhere (as discussed later)
    - For every valid pair of clicks (i.e. those that satisfy game rules), the layout is modified.

Objects:

We will distribute the code among the following objects (sprites):

- The "Square" sprite will contain logic to draw the visible 4x4 grid.
- The "Frontend" object will contain common code for all chess pieces.
- 5 chess objects: For each chess piece we will have a separate object containing its own logic – which would be fairly similar to each other.
- "Undo" sprite for the click button
- "Backend" will contain logic to manipulate the 4x4 board (i.e. the 16-item list) as per the game rules. This object (sprite) will drive the entire game.

We will add methods (procedures/scripts) to these objects as we process each feature idea below.

We may also add more objects as we learn more about the features of the program.

Global data:

List "L": 16 items, will hold the current status of the board, 0 for empty cell, r/b/q/k/p (for the respective chess piece)

Integers "from" and "to": locations (1 to 16) for each move

Integer "clicked": the most recent cell (1 to 16) that was clicked

Feature Idea # 1: The chess board

Draw a 4x4 grid of chess-like cells.

Design:

As mentioned above, we will simply borrow an older program called "Chessboard" (from the book "Practice CS Concepts with Snap") and modify it to draw only a 4x4 layout. Since the chessboard itself does not have to be sensitive to user clicks, (in this game, user can only click on chess pieces), we don't need to use clones to draw the chessboard.

Feature Idea # 2: The initial setup

When green flag is clicked, the game should display the initial board positions.

Design:

The game obviously depends on an initial layout. We will use a collection of possible layouts (copied from the actual board game). Each layout could be encoded into a 16-letter string: 0 for blank cell and r/k/q/b/p for a chess piece. For example, the encoding for the board shown below would be "00q000r0k0000p00".

We will have 4 collections of such encoded layouts based on level of difficulty: Expert, Advanced, Intermediate, and Beginner.

We could save these 4 collections in 4 separate variables: one for each type. So, for example, "expert_string" would contain all expert-level layouts separated by commas. Since Snap saves variable contents in its projects, we don't need to load these strings every time we run the program.

We will need 4 additional sprites (click buttons) to allow the user to pick a level by clicking. The program would then take the appropriate comma-separated string, split it into a list, and pick one of the layouts at random. This layout encoding (16-letter string) would then result into the actual chess layout as described in the next feature.

Feature Idea # 2: Layout of chess pieces

Display chess pieces according to the current layout.

Design:

The current layout, as described above is a 16-letter string. We will split it into a 16-item list L. This list will henceforth determine what each board position looks like (either blank or with a chess piece). The "frontend" object will scan this list and inform (by sending messages) the chess pieces to show up at their assigned places. This scanning script can simply broadcast the letter associated with the piece.

Since each piece can have 2 instances (i.e. 2 rooks, 2 pawns, etc.) we will use clones of each piece. The clone, when it receive the message (e.g. "r" for the rook), will create and place a clone at the same position as in L (e.g. if "r" appears at position 12 in L, the rook clone will appear at position 12 in the 4x4 grid).

How will the piece calculate its X and Y coordinate? Since the X and Y of the board's upper-left corner are fixed, we can use the following formulae to do the calculation:

X = xcorner + [cell size x remainder of ((cell id − 1) / 4)]
Y = ycorner − [cell size x integer division of (floor cell id − 1) and 4]

Feature Idea # 3: The move

When user clicks on two pieces, make the first piece replace the second. (*Do not check the validity of the move.*)

Design:

According to the game's rules, every move involves one chess piece taking another. Thus, we have a 2-step transaction here: in step 1, user clicks on a piece, and in step 2, they click either on the same piece (to cancel the move) or on another piece to take it. How can we program this? How do we know whether a click is the 1st or 2nd click? Here is one possible approach.

When a piece is clicked it will simply save its grid location (1 to 16) in a global variable ("clicked") and inform the backend.

The backend will use two global variables: "from" and "to". Initially "from" would have some invalid value such as -1 to indicate that the user is yet to begin the move. As soon as user makes the first click, we save the location in "from". The second time user clicks, "from" would not be -1, so we will know this is the second click. If the second click is the same as the first, we simply cancel the move by setting "from" back to -1.

Otherwise, we do the following:
1. Validate the move: Send a message to the piece at the first click to check if the move is valid (this feature is implemented later). Proceed only if true.
2. Save the move in an "undo" list (for the "undo" feature implemented later).
3. Update list L to show the move.
4. Send a message to the piece at the second click to inform it to pack its bags (since it is getting killed)
5. Send a message to the piece at the first click to inform it to move to the second click.

Each chess piece object will implement its own logic for steps 1, 4, and 5 as follows:
- For Step 1, each piece will implement a "ValidateMove" method (script), which will verify that the intended move is legal (e.g. rook can only move straight). If it is not, this method will return error to the backend which should then cancel the move by setting "from" back to -1. We will implement this method later and for now we will assume the user knows what they are doing.

- For step 4, each piece will implement a "Die" method which will cause the clone to delete itself.
- For step 5, each piece will implement a "Move" method which will cause the clone to move to the specified "to" position.

Save as Program Version 1

Congratulations! You have completed all the basic features of the game. Compare your program with my program in the file below.

File: solochess-1.xml

How to play the game:
1. Click the "Green flag".
2. Pick one of the levels of expertise. The initial layout will be shown.
3. Play the game by following the instructions on the left side.

Feature Idea # 4: Undo

User should be able to undo his/her moves.

Design:

For this, we will need to save every move – the best place would be a list. Let us call it "undoL" – the undo list. We will save in a single string both the "from" and "to" locations as well as which piece was taken (killed) by which piece, for example, "2,15,k,p" would mean knight at 2 was moved to replace a pawn at 15.

Next, we will provide an "Undo" click button. When user clicks this button, the latest element in "undoL" would be popped and processed. For example, if it is "2,15,k,p", we need to perform the following actions to undo:
- The knight at 15 came from 2, so we will ask it to move back to 2 (using the "Move" method).
- A new pawn needs to appear at 15. A pawn clone can be created and placed the same way as during the initial placement (backend will send a "p" message).

Of course, don't forget to update list L with the new layout since pieces have moved around.

Feature Idea # 5: Help

Provide a help screen.

Design:

This is a straightforward task. Create a "Help" sprite and display it first when Green flag is clicked. You will need to ensure all other characters/sprites hide at this time. When the user clicks to continue, hide the "help" sprite and continue the program.

Save as Program Version 2

Congratulations! You have completed the undo feature of the game. Compare your program with my program in the file below.

File: solochess-2.xml

Feature Idea # 6: Allow valid moves

In feature idea #3 above, we move pieces without checking if the moves follow chess rules. Implement these rules. For example, bishops only travel diagonally.

Design:

This feature would be implemented by each piece separately (as the "ValidateMove" method) since the rules of movement are unique to each piece.

Step 1: ***Ensure pawn moves are valid.***

Design:

Although pawns move straight up only, while killing they move diagonally. Consider the board as shown below:

In this layout, the pawn can kill the rook or the bishop, but not the knight or any other piece on the board (if there were any). How do we check that the move picked by the user ("from" to "to") is valid?

After careful analysis, we come up with the following observations:
1. "from" is always greater than "to"
2. "from" cannot be less than 5
3. "to" cannot be greater than 12
4. The difference between them can either be 3 or 5.
5. When the difference is 3, "from" cannot be in the last column
6. When the difference is 5, "to" cannot be in the last column

The following algorithm takes care of all these observations. Since we only allow a gap of 3 or 5, items 1 thru 4 are automatically taken care of. (For example, if from = 4 (violating #2) and to = 1, the gap would be 3 and the first "if" below would be violated.)

Algorithm IsMoveValidPawn for the pawn:
```
Input: from and to (numbers 1 to 16)
Gap = from - to
If Gap is 3 AND "from" is not in the last column
            Return True
End if
If Gap is 5 AND "to" is not in the last column
            Return True
End if
Return false
```

  | *Adventures in Snap Programming*

Step 2: *Ensure knight moves are valid.*

Design:

Knight can move as follows:
- Pick any of the 4 directions (north/south/east/west)
- Move 2 steps straight
- Move 1 step at the right angle

In the layout above the knight can move to 1, 3, 8, or 16. How do we check that the move picked by the user ("from" to "to") is valid?

After careful analysis, we come up with the following observations:
- It is better to use row (R) and column (C) to do this check.
- There are 8 possible movements as below. (Not all would be valid)
- New positions if it moved 2 steps east, 1 step north or south: $(R-1,C+2)$, $(R+1,C+2)$
- New positions if it moved 2 steps west, 1 step north or south: $(R-1,C-2)$, $(R+1,C-2)$
- New positions if it moved 2 steps north, 1 step east or west: $(R+2,C+1)$, $(R+2,C-1)$
- New positions if it moved 2 steps south, 1 step east or west: $(R-2,C+1)$, $(R-2,C-1)$

- If we removed the invalid positions (by looking at the new row and column values and checking if they are in the range 1 to 16) we would have a list of valid moves
- We could then check if "to" is one of the valid moves (i.e. there is a piece to kill)

The following algorithm takes care of these observations.

```
Algorithm IsMoveValidKnight for the knight:
Input: from and to (numbers 1 to 16)
R = calculate row # of "to"
C = calculate col # of "to"
Create a list L of all valid moves as described above
      Example: (R-1, C+2) is a possible move
      If R-1 is a valid row and C+2 is a valid column
            newposition = ((R-1)-1) * 4 + (C+2)
            Add newposition to L
      End if
If "to" is a member of L return True, else return False
```

**Step 3**: Ensure bishop moves are valid.

Design:
Bishop can move as follows:
- Pick any of the 4 diagonal directions (nw/sw/se/sw)
- Move straight until it hits another piece

In the above layout, the bishop can legally move to position 4 and any other move would be invalid (for this game). How do we check that the move picked by the user ("from" to "to") is valid?

After careful analysis, we come up with the following observations:
-   If "from" and "to" are diagonally positioned (newrow – oldrow must be the same in value as newcolumn – oldcolumn) it is a valid move.
-   Next we need to find in which direction "to" is situated. This can be found by comparing row/column of "to" with those of "from". For example, if newrow < oldrow and newcolumn < oldcolumn, "to" must be northwest of "from".
-   We find the first valid cell (i.e. occupied) in that direction. If it is the same as "to" it is a valid move, else it's an invalid move.

The following algorithm takes care of these observations.

```
Algorithm IsMoveValidBishop for the bishop:
Input: from and to (numbers 1 to 16)
R1 and C1: calculate row/column of "from" (1 to 4)
R2 and C2: calculate row/column of "to" (1 to 4)
g1 = R2 - R1
g2 = C2 - C1
If value of g1 and g2 are not equal return False
Determine "direction" of the move by comparing g1 and g2.
     For example: If g1<0 and g2<0 the direction is Northwest.
For each direction:
     Imagine bishop moving from "from" one cell at a time.
     Move until an occupied cell is found.
     If occupied cell same as "to" return True
     Else return False
End for
```

Step 4: Ensure rook moves are valid.

Design:
Rook can move as follows:
-   Pick any of the 4 standard directions (N/E/W/S)
-   Move straight until it hits another piece

In the above layout, the rook at 13 can legally move to positions 1 and 15 and any other move would be invalid (for this game). How do we check that the move picked by the user ("from" to "to") is valid?

After careful analysis, we come up with the following observations:
-   If "from" and "to" are positioned straight up/down or sideways (both newrow – oldrow and newcolumn – oldcolumn cannot be non-zero) it is a valid move.
-   Next we need to find in which direction "to" is situated. This can be found by comparing row/column of "to" with those of "from". For example, if newrow < oldrow and newcolumn = oldcolumn, "to" must be North of "from".
-   We find the first valid cell (i.e. occupied) in that direction. If it is the same as "to" it is a valid move, else it's an invalid move.

The following algorithm takes care of these observations.

```
Algorithm IsMoveValidRook for the rook:
Input: from and to (numbers 1 to 16)
R1 and C1: calculate row/column of "from" (1 to 4)
R2 and C2: calculate row/column of "to" (1 to 4)
g1 = R2 - R1
g2 = C2 - C1
Only one of g1 and g2 must be non-zero. If not, return False
Determine "direction" of the move by comparing g1 and g2.
      For example: If g1=0 and g2<0 the direction is West.
```

 | *Adventures in Snap Programming*

```
For each direction:
    Imagine rook moving from "from" one cell at a time.
    Move until an occupied cell is found.
    If occupied cell same as "to" return True
    Else return False
End for
```

Step 5*: Ensure queen moves are valid.*

Design:

Queen can move either as a rook or as a bishop. So we can simply use the bishop and rook algorithms designed earlier.

```
We first run the bishop algorithm
    If it returns True, we return True
Next, we run the rook algorithm and return whatever it returns.
```

Save as Program Version 3

Congratulations! You have completed all features listed so far of the game. Compare your program with my program in the file below.

File: solochess-3.xml

How to play the game:

1. Click the "Green flag". Read help and then click to continue.
2. Pick one of the levels of expertise. The initial layout will be shown.
3. Play the game by following the instructions on the left side. Click "Undo" to retract a move. You can perform undo multiple times.

Feature Idea # 7: Automation: Computer solves the board

In the "auto" mode, the computer should attempt to solve the current board. User should be able to start the auto mode any time during the play.

Design:

This interesting feature is also the most challenging. We will need to think what it means to automate the game-play.

Consider how a user would play in the manual mode. He/she would be presented with a board and will pick a move (i.e. a piece that can kill another). After this move has been made, he/she is presented with a modified board and may undo the previous move or once again make another move. Thus, you can see the same 2 steps repeated again and again until the game is over. So, we could create a "recursive" approach in which the user would make the "first possible move" – i.e. scan the board from the top-left and look for a piece that can kill another piece. As soon as such a move is found, he/she will make it and then make the recursive call (i.e. present the user with the new board). If the recursive call returns "failure" -- which means the board that we created did not lead to a solution, we will undo the previous move (because that move indeed got us into an intractable position) and make the "next possible move" and try again. If we exhaust all possible moves with the current board, we return "failure".

This approach is called "brute force" or "exhaustive search" because we indeed try all possible moves until gold is struck. This recursive process will drive the automation.

Here is the algorithm for the main recursive method:

```
Algorithm PlayGameAuto
Input: board (our 16-item list)
For every piece on the board:
      Build a list of possible moves for this piece
      For every move in this list of moves:
            Make the move and update the board
            If only 1 piece left:
                  Declare victory and return "success"
            End if
            return value = Recursive call with the modified board
            If return value indicates success:
                  No need to proceed, so return success
            End if
            If return value indicates failure
                  Current board did not work, so undo the move
                  and continue to the next move
            End if
      End For
End For
No more pieces, return "failure"
```

 | *Adventures in Snap Programming*

Here are a couple of important details of this recursive process that need further work:

In Step 2, we need a list of valid moves for the given piece. (In the manual mode, the user visually decides the "valid" moves for a piece.) We will need each piece (rook, etc.) to provide a method to give a list of possible legal moves from a specific position. This method (custom block) would have to be "public" (accessible to all sprites) since it would be called by the "backend" sprite. Here is a list of the new methods:

```
Algorithm GetValidMoves
This method will call other methods below.
Input: cell (board position 1 to 16)
Steps:
Depending on which piece occupies "cell", call the appropriate Get**
method.
```

```
Algorithm GetValidMovesKnight
Input: cell (board position 1 to 16)
Steps:
For every occupied position "p" on the board check if a knight can
legally move from "cell" to "p". We will use the IsMoveValidKnight
algorithm designed earlier.
Make a list of all such valid "p"s and return it.
```

The remaining algorithms (listed below) will use an identical approach.
```
GetValidMovesPawn
GetValidMovesBishop
GetValidMovesRook
GetValidMovesQueen
```

In the manual mode, each move consists of two clicks. In automation, no clicks are required, so we can directly pick two moves and supply them to the backend logic to process.

Finally, before we run the automated algorithm, we should undo all the moves made by the user thus far. This is a straightforward matter since we already have an "undo" script. See the steps below:

```
Repeat until Undo list is empty
     Send "undo" message
End repeat
```

Save as Program Final Version

Congratulations! You have completed the automation feature of the game. Compare your program with my program at the link below.

File: solochess-final.xml

Published at Berkeley site: Solo Chess
(`https://snap.berkeley.edu/snap/snap.html#present:Username=abjoshi&ProjectName=Solo%20chess`)

How to play the game:

1. Click the "Green flag". Read help and then click to continue.
2. Pick one of the levels of expertise. The initial layout will be shown.
3. Play the game by following the instructions on the left side. Click "Undo" to retract a move. You can perform undo multiple times.
4. Press "s" any time during game-play to make the computer try to finish the remaining game.

He who knows it not, and can no longer wonder, no longer feel amazement, is as good as dead.
– Hans Selye

Program description

This is an interesting graphic in which a chessboard-like layout appears as if it has been stretched in the center, or it is being viewed from a lens of some sort. See below:

In reality, there is no stretching at all; it is a trick played on our eyes by the arrangement of the tiny squares inside the chessboard.

So, our task in this project is to essentially draw the above design. We should attempt to draw it using only two sprites (or costumes): a black and a white square.

Explore the program:

If you want to play with my final program to get a feel for this optical illusion, click the link specified at the end of the chapter. Try not to peek at the scripts yet, since we want to design them ourselves below.

Steps to run the program:

1. Click the Green flag.
2. Follow the prompts.

Snap and CS Concepts Used

When we design this program, we will make use of the following Snap and CS concepts. Learn these concepts if you don't know them before proceeding further.

- Algorithms
    - Designing new algorithms
- Arithmetic
    - Expressions
    - Basic operators (+, -, x, /)
    - Advanced operators: mod, floor, etc.
- Concurrency:
    - Synchronization using broadcasting
- Conditional statements:
    - Conditions: YES/NO questions
    - Relational operators (=, <, >)
    - Conditionals (IF)
    - Conditionals (If-Else)
    - Conditionals (nested IF)
    - Boolean operators (and, or, not)
- Data structures – list
    - List operations: add, insert, replace, remove, scan

- o   Using list as 2-D array
- o   Advanced list processing
- Data types – basic
  - o   Integers
- Data types – strings
  - o   String operations
- Looping (iteration)
  - o   Looping - simple (repeat, for)
  - o   Looping - nested
  - o   Looping - conditional (repeat until)
- OOP
  - o   Clones
- Pen Art
  - o   Stamp
- Procedures
  - o   User defined (custom)
  - o   Procedures with parameters and return value
- Program output
  - o   Text
  - o   GUI (sprites)
- Random numbers
- Sequence
- User input
  - o   Text
  - o   Click buttons
- User interface elements
  - o   Sprites and costumes
  - o   Buttons
  - o   Clones
- Variables
  - o   Simple
  - o   Local/global scope
  - o   Script variables

High Level Design

As usual, let us take a step back and think about the big pieces of this program.

The first obvious step is to draw the chessboard-like layout. If you look carefully, it is not the usual 8x8 design, but a 9x9 design.

The next step is to figure out how to draw the tiny squares. One idea would be to develop a general-purpose algorithm to draw 4 tiny squares in the 4 corners of any square. This algorithm could then be modified to control, via an input parameter, which of those squares gets drawn. This input parameter could be a bit pattern, such as, "1010" in which 1 means the square is to be drawn and 0 means it is not.

Finally, we could set up a static list of 'bit patterns' which will tell us the expected "tiny square layout" for each and every cell of the chessboard.

Let us first design the data structures (i.e. data types and variables that will hold all the important information).

Data structures:
- Patterns (string): a comma-separated list of 81 strings (because there are 81 cells in the chessboard), each string is 4 letter long (e.g. 1010) and is the bit pattern for the corresponding cell in the chessboard. "Patterns" is a fixed string since we are going to draw only one chessboard layout.

- Bits (list): list of bit patterns (obtained from "Patterns" using the split operator)

Feature Idea # 1: The pseudo-chess board

Draw a 9x9 grid of chess-like cells.

Design:
For this, we will simply borrow an older program called *"Chessboard"* (from the book "Practice CS Concepts with Snap") and modify it to draw the 9x9 layout. We will use STAMP to draw the chessboard.

Feature Idea # 2: Tiny squares

Write a script that can draw 4 tiny squares in the 4 corners of a bigger square.

Design:

Let us do this in 2 steps:

Step 1: Draw the following pattern:

We already have 2 costumes for the white and black squares. Now we need an algorithm to draw smaller squares in the 4 corners of the bigger square. We will assume that the bigger square is already there and the costume has been switched to the opposite color. One idea is to jump to the 4 corners one by one, stamp, and return to the center. See the diagram below:

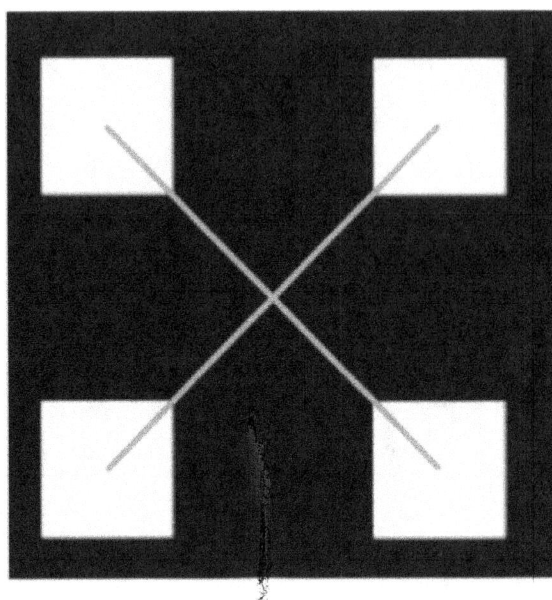

The purple lines indicate how the smaller square can jump from corner to corner.

Here is the algorithm:

```
Algorithm Tiny Squares
Resize to 1/4th original size
Calculate distance "d" from center to any one of the corners
Point towards any corner
Repeat 4
      Move d steps
      Stamp
      Move back d steps
      Turn 90
End repeat
Restore size and orientation
```

Step 2: Control which squares will be drawn.

We will modify the above algorithm by supplying an input parameter that contains a bit pattern, e.g. 1010. Starting with the square in the northwest corner and going clockwise, this parameter will determine which tiny squares would be visible.

```
Algorithm Tiny Squares
Input parameter: Bits
Resize to 1/4th original size
Calculate distance "d" from center to any one of the corners
Point towards NW corner
I = 1
Repeat 4
      Move d steps
      If I'th bit in Bits is 1
            Stamp
      End if
      I = I + 1
      Move back d steps
      Turn 90
End repeat
Restore size and orientation
```

Save as Program Version 1

Congratulations! You have completed the most basic features listed above. Compare your program with my program in the file below.

File: chessboard-stretch-1.xml

How to play the game:

1. Click the Green flag. The 9x9 chessboard design will be drawn.
2. Press SPACE to draw the 4 tiny squares pattern.

Feature Idea # 3: Stretch the chessboard

Stretch the chess board as shown in the figure at the top of this chapter.

Design:

Here is the complete picture once again.

The remaining work involves drawing the tiny squares as shown in this picture. We already have a way to draw 4 tiny squares in a bigger square by using a bit pattern. Can we extend this idea for the final figure?

Here is one way we can do it. There are a total of 81 cells in this figure. We can imagine that each of these cells has some pattern of the tiny squares. See some examples below. The bit pattern describes which tiny squares are visible as seen clockwise starting from the NW corner.

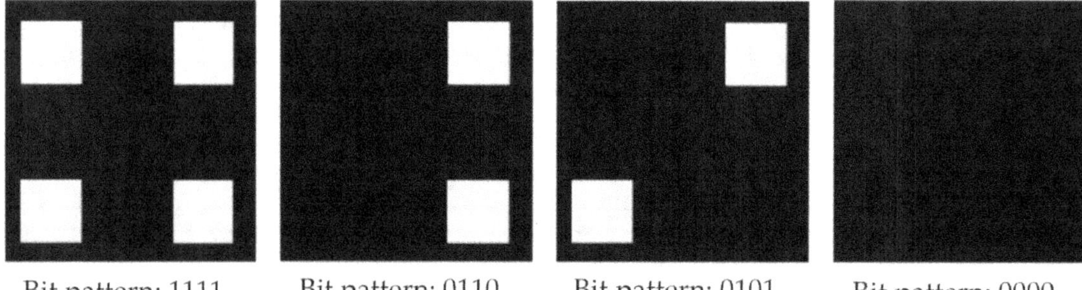

Bit pattern: 1111   Bit pattern: 0110   Bit pattern: 0101   Bit pattern: 0000

But, how about drawing tiny black squares in white cells? Well, we will let each cell figure it out by looking at its own color. The bit patterns would still be the same.

So, we could have a list of such bit patterns for the entire 9x9 chessboard. Here are all the 81 bit patterns for our optical illusion, which we will save in a list.

```
0000,0000,0000,0000,0000,0000,0000,0000,0000,
0000,0000,0000,0101,0011,1010,0000,0000,0000,
0000,0000,0101,0101,0011,1010,1010,0000,0000,
0000,0101,0101,0101,0011,1010,1010,1010,0000,
0000,0110,0110,0110,0000,1001,1001,1001,0000,
0000,1010,1010,1010,1100,0101,0101,0101,0000,
0000,0000,1010,1010,1100,0101,0101,0000,0000,
0000,0000,0000,1010,1100,0101,0000,0000,0000,
0000,0000,0000,0000,0000,0000,0000,0000,0000,

Bits = [ "0000", "0000", …, "0101", …, "1010", …, "0000" ]
```

And then, we will have a script that runs through this list and draws tiny squares in each cell according to that cell's bit pattern.

Here is the algorithm:

```
Algorithm draw optical illusion:
Input: "Bits" – list of 81 bit patterns
Pick the white costume (since the first cell is black)
I = 1
Go to first cell
Repeat 81
      Bit pattern BP = I'th item in Bits
      Call algorithm "draw tiny squares" with input BP
      Move to next cell
      Change costume
      I = I + 1
End repeat
```

Save the final version

Congratulations! You have completed all the features of the optical illusion. Compare your program with my program in the file below.

File: chessboard-stretch-2.xml

Berkeley website: Chess board stretch

```
(https://snap.berkeley.edu/snap/snap.html#present:Username=abjoshi&ProjectName
=chessboard-stretch-2)
```

How to run the program:
1. Click the Green flag.
2. Follow the prompts.

Bonus Project 2: Missing Digit

When you learn, teach. When you get, give.
– Maya Angelou

Program description

This program is actually a simulation of a game played between two friends. Compared to most of the earlier projects in this book, this is a much simpler program to write. What is interesting about it is that you can use it as a framework for many similar conversations between friends related to "mathematical magic".

Let's say there are two friends Leila and Sheila. Leila tells Sheila that she is a detective who can trace missing numbers.

Leila asks Sheila to write down any string of numbers without showing you the result. (For example, Sheila writes 714329167.)
Next, Leila asks Sheila to add a zero to the right.
(New number would be 7143291670)
Next, she asks Sheila to subtract her first number.
(7143291670 - 714329167 = 6428962503)
Finally Leila tells Sheila to remove any digit except 0 from the number she is left with.
(Sheila eliminates 4. Her remaining number will be 628962503.)

Leila now states that if Sheila will show her just her remaining number, she will tell Sheila what digit she eliminated – that she will find the missing digit.

What is the trick:

Here is how Leila finds the missing digit. First, she adds the digits in the remaining number Sheila gives her. She keeps adding until she is left with a single digit.
In the above example:
-    Adding all digits in 628962503 gives 41.

- Add all digits in 41 gives 5.

If this single digit is 9, that's the answer. Otherwise, Leila subtracts this digit from 9 to get the missing digit.

Explore the game:

If you want to play with my final program to get a feel for this game, import into Snap the link given at the end of the chapter. Try not to peek at the scripts yet, since we want to design them ourselves below.

1. Click the "Green flag".
2. Pick between interactive and animation modes. In "interactive" mode you play the role of Sheila. In "animation" mode you just watch the simulated game.

Snap and CS Concepts Used

When we design this program, we will make use of the following Snap and CS concepts. Learn these concepts if you don't know them before proceeding further.

- Algorithms
- Conditions: YES/NO questions
- Conditionals (If-Else)
- Conditionals (IF)
- Data types – numbers
- Data types – strings
- Data types – String operations (join, letter, length of)
- Data types – string traversal
- Events
- Looping – simple (repeat, forever)
- Looping – nested
- Looping – conditional
- Procedures – custom, with parameters and return value
- Random numbers
- Relational operators (<, >, =)
- Sequence
- Synchronization using broadcasting
- User input – text

- Variables
- Variables - local/global scope

High Level Design

In the animation mode, the program involves a conversation between two sprites which can be implemented using broadcasting. Leila would send a broadcast every time she expects Sheila to respond in some way. Sheila would receive each such broadcast and perform the expected action.

Since Leila is not supposed to know the numbers Sheila is working on, Sheila must use variables with "local scope", i.e. her variables must be private (created "for this sprite only").

Let's consider each exchange of the conversation as a feature idea and go through the entire conversation.

In the interactive mode, the user (you) plays the role of Sheila and does all the calculations.

Feature Idea # 1: Pick a large number

Leila asks Sheila to pick a large number.

Design:

Sheila uses the "pick random" operator and saves the result in a private variable "n1".

Feature Idea # 2: Add zero

Leila asks Sheila to attach a 0 at the end.

Design:

Sheila uses the "join" operator, or multiplies n1 by 10 and saves the result in a private variable "n2".

Feature Idea # 3: Subtract

Leila asks Sheila to subtract the original number from this larger number.

Design:

Sheila subtracts n2 from n1 and saves the result in a private variable "n3".

Feature Idea # 4: Remove any digit

Leila tells Sheila to remove any digit except 0 from the number she is left with.

Step 1: Pick a non-zero digit from n3 at random.

Design:

We can use "repeat until" and call "pick random" until a non-zero digit is picked from n3.

Step 2: Remove the non-zero digit from n3 and save the result in a private variable "n4".

Design:

Using an example would help here. Let's say n3 = 60174615 and the selected digit is 1. In this case there are two "1"s and we will pick the first. We need to remove 1 and save 6074615 into n4.

This can be achieved by the following algorithm:
String 1 = string to the left of "1" excluding "1" of course. (In this example: 60)
String 2 = string to the right of "1" excluding "1". (In this example: 74615).
Join string 1 and 2 and save the result in n4. (In this example n4 = 6074615).

Use "string traversal" to achieve all steps above.

Feature Idea # 5: Show

Leila now states that if Sheila will show her just her remaining number, she will tell Sheila what digit she removed.

Design:

So far, all numbers of Sheila are being stored in private variables. This time, Sheila will copy n4 to a global variable "N".

Feature Idea # 6: Guess

Leila should now be able to guess the missing digit by looking at the number N.

Design:

Here is how you find the missing digit. First, add the digits in the remaining number. Keep adding until you are left with a single digit.

Let's say the remaining number is 628962503.
- Adding all digits in 628962503 gives 41.
- Add all digits in 41 gives 5.

Subtract this digit from 9. That will give you the missing number.

To add up all digits, we can use the standard "string traversal" algorithm. But, we need to repeat this process until we get a single digit. "Repeat until" can come to rescue here.

Feature Idea # 7: Interactive mode

In the interactive mode, the user plays the role of Sheila.

Step 1: Provide the option to run the program in "interactive" and "animation" modes.

Design:

This is a simple matter of providing two click-buttons which are shown at the beginning of the program. If "interactive" is clicked, Leila talks with the user, if "animation" is clicked, she talks with Sheila as before.

Step 2: Convert the script that computes the missing digit into a custom block since the same code is run for both modes.

Design:

This is a simple matter of creating a custom block called FindMissingDigit. It will take a number as input and return the digit. It will use local script variables for internal calculations.

Save as Program Version "Final"

Congratulations! You have completed all the main features of the game. Compare your program with my program at the link below.

File: missing-digit.xml
Berkeley Snap website: Missing digit
(`https://snap.berkeley.edu/snapsource/snap.html#present:Username=abjoshi&Proje ctName=missing-digit`)

How to play the game:

1. Click the "Green flag".
2. Pick between interactive and animation modes. In "interactive" mode you play the role of Sheila. In "animation" mode you just watch the simulated game.